Contents

Nonfiction Reading Practice Is Important

Research indicates that more than 80 percent of what people read and write is nonfiction text. Newspapers, magazines, directions on new products, application forms, and how-to manuals are just some of the types of nonfiction reading material we encounter on a daily basis. As students move through the grades, an increasing amount of time is spent reading expository text for subjects such as science and social studies. Most reading comprehension sections on state and national tests are nonfiction.

Each Unit Has...

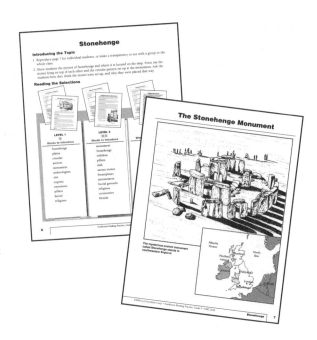

A Teacher Resource Page

Vocabulary words for all three levels are given. The vocabulary lists include proper nouns and content-specific terms, as well as other challenging words.

A Visual Aid

The visual aid represents the topic for the unit. It is intended to build interest in the topic. Reproduce the visual on an overhead transparency or photocopy it for each student.

Articles at Three Reading Levels

Each unit presents three articles on the same topic. The articles progress in difficulty from easiest (Level 1) to hardest (Level 3). An icon indicates the level of the article—Level 1 (■), Level 2 (■ ■), Level 3 (■ ■ ■). Each article contains new vocabulary and ideas to incorporate into classroom discussion. The Level 1 article gives readers a core vocabulary and a basic understanding of the topic. More challenging vocabulary words are used as the level of the article increases. Interesting details also change or increase in the Levels 2 and 3 articles.

Level 1

Level 2

Level 3

Readability

All of the articles in this series have been edited for readability. Readability formulas, which are mathematical calculations, are considered to be one way of predicting reading ease. The Flesch-Kincaid and Fry Graph formulas were used to check for readability. These formulas count and factor in three variables: the number of words, syllables, and sentences in a passage to determine the reading level. When appropriate, proper nouns and content-specific terms were discounted in determining readability levels for the articles in this book.

Nonfiction Reading Practice, Grade 5 • EMC 3316 • ©2003 by Evan-Moor Corp.

Student Comprehension Pages

A vocabulary/comprehension page follows each article. There are five multiple-choice questions that provide practice with the types of questions that are generally used on standardized reading tests. The bonus question is intended to elicit higher-level thinking skills.

Level 1

Level 2

Level 3

Additional Resources

Six graphic organizers to extend comprehension are also included in the book. (See page 4 for suggestions for use.)

Biography Sketch

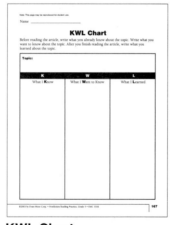

KWL Chart

Making an Outline

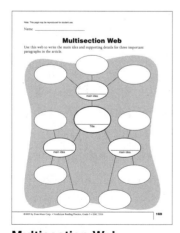

Multisection Web

Sequence Chart

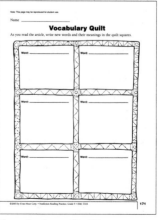

Vocabulary Quilt

How to Use *Nonfiction Reading Practice*

Planning Guided Reading Instruction

The units in this book do not need to be taught in sequential order. Choose the units that align with your curriculum or with student interests.

- For whole-group instruction, introduce the unit to the total class. Provide each student with an article at the appropriate reading level. Guide students as they read the articles. You may want to have students read with partners. Then conduct a class discussion to share the different information learned.

- For small-group instruction, choose an article at the appropriate reading level for each group. The group reads the article with teacher guidance and discusses the information presented.

- The articles may also be used to assist readers in moving from less difficult to more challenging reading material. After building vocabulary and familiarity with the topic at the appropriate level, students may be able to successfully read the article at the next level of difficulty.

Presenting a Unit

1. Before reading the articles, make an overhead transparency of the visual aid or reproduce it for individual student use. Use the visual to engage student interest in the topic, present vocabulary, and build background that will aid in comprehension. This step is especially important for visual learners.

2. Present vocabulary that may be difficult to decode or understand. A list of suggested vocabulary words for each article is given on the teacher resource page. Where possible, connect these words to the visual aid.

3. Present and model several appropriate reading strategies that aid in comprehension of the expository text. You may wish to make an overhead transparency of the reading strategies checklist on page 5 or reproduce it for students to refer to as they read.

4. You may want to use one of the graphic organizers provided on pages 166–171. Make an overhead transparency, copy the organizer onto the board or chart paper, or reproduce it for students. Record information learned to help students process and organize the information.

5. Depending on the ability levels of the students, the comprehension/vocabulary pages may be completed as a group or as independent practice. It is always advantageous to share and discuss answers as a group so that students correct misconceptions. An answer key is provided at the back of this book.

Nonfiction Reading Practice, Grade 5 • EMC 3316 • ©2003 by Evan-Moor Corp.

Name _____

Reading Checklist

Directions: Check off the reading hints that you use to understand the story.

Before I Read

_____ I think about what I already know.

_____ I think about what I want to learn.

_____ I predict what is going to happen.

_____ I read the title for clues.

_____ I look at the pictures and read the captions for extra clues.

_____ I skim the article to read headings and words in bold or italic print.

_____ I read over the comprehension questions for the article.

While I Read

_____ I ask questions and read for answers.

_____ I reread parts that are confusing.

_____ I reread the captions under the pictures.

_____ I make mental pictures as I read.

_____ I use context clues to understand difficult words.

_____ I take notes when I am reading.

_____ I underline important key words and phrases.

After I Read

_____ I think about what I have just read.

_____ I speak, draw, and write about what I read.

_____ I confirm or change the predictions I made.

_____ I reread to find the main idea.

_____ I reread to find details.

_____ I read the notes I took as I read.

_____ I look back at the article to find answers to questions.

Stonehenge

Introducing the Topic

1. Reproduce page 7 for individual students, or make a transparency to use with a group or the whole class.

2. Show students the picture of Stonehenge and where it is located on the map. Point out the stones lying on top of each other and the circular pattern set up at the monument. Ask the students how they think the stones were set up, and why they were placed that way.

Reading the Selections

LEVEL 1
■

Words to Introduce

Stonehenge

plains

circular

ancient

monument

archeologists

site

experts

enormous

pillars

burial

religious

LEVEL 2
■ ■

Words to Introduce

monument

Stonehenge

trilithon

pillars

slab

sarsen stones

breastplates

astronomers

burial grounds

religious

ceremonies

Druids

LEVEL 3
■ ■ ■

Words to Introduce

ancient

monument

Stonehenge

historians

phases

diameter

sarsen stones

trilithon

lintel

horizontal

The Stonehenge Monument

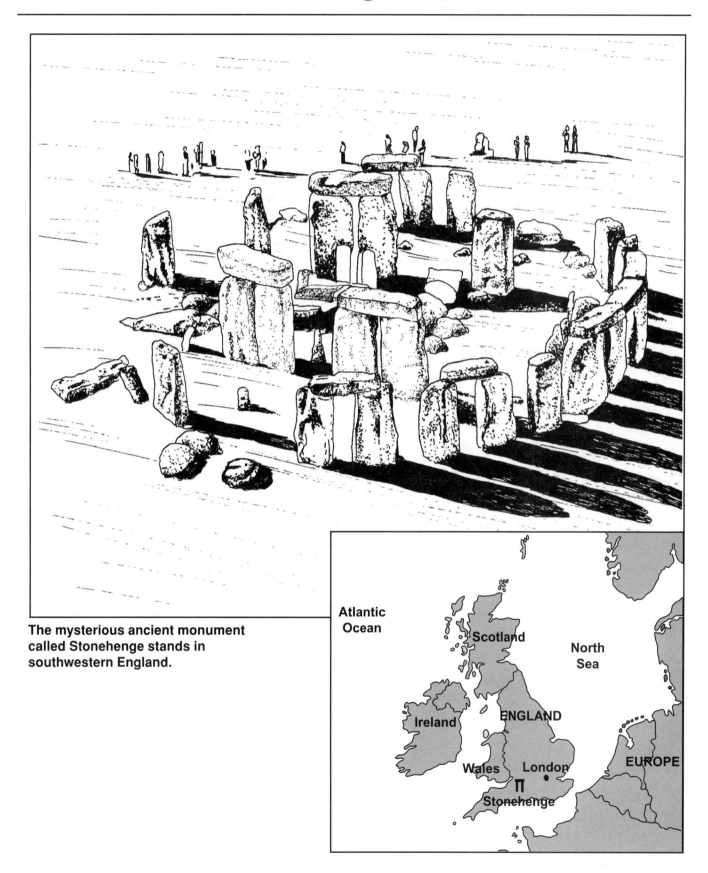

The mysterious ancient monument called Stonehenge stands in southwestern England.

The Mystery of Stonehenge

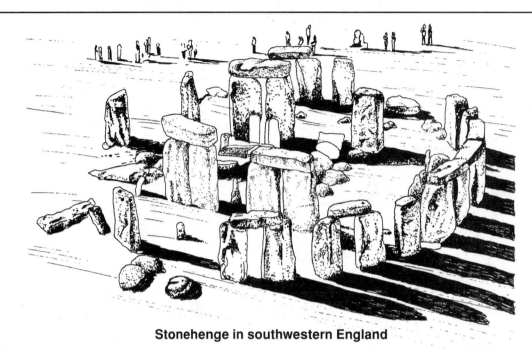

Stonehenge in southwestern England

Imagine walking along the plains of southwestern England. Suddenly, you come upon a group of rocks sticking up from the ground. The giant rocks are set up in a circular pattern. Some rocks appear to be lying on top of rocks set up like posts. You wonder how the rocks were placed that way.

Ancient Monument

Such a monument really exists. The ancient monument is called Stonehenge. Stonehenge means "hanging stones." The monument consists of a group of gigantic stones. Archeologists believe the stones date back almost 5,000 years ago. The rough-cut stones are set in a circular pattern. Some of the stones are missing, but archeologists figured out what the monument looked like when it was built.

Gigantic Stones

Archeologists think that ancient people built the monument starting about 2800 B.C. Hundreds of men hauled gigantic stones to the site. Experts believe men pulled these enormous stones with ropes to move them. Some of the heavy stones weighed about 50 tons (45 metric tonnes). Experts think they were moved in the winter. The stones could be slid across ice and snow. The stones were brought to the site and propped up to make pillars.

It's a Mystery!

People visiting Stonehenge wonder why the stones were set up this way. There are many ideas, but no one knows for sure. Some people think it was a burial ground. Others think Stonehenge was a religious site. Still others think Stonehenge told the passing of the seasons.

The reason why Stonehenge was built remains a mystery. A million tourists visit this place each year to try to uncover the mystery of Stonehenge.

Name _____

The Mystery of Stonehenge

Fill in the bubble to answer each question or complete each sentence.

1. Stonehenge is _____.
   - Ⓐ an ancient stone monument
   - Ⓑ an ancient rock
   - Ⓒ a circular stone
   - Ⓓ an archeologist

2. Stonehenge is located in which country?
   - Ⓐ United States
   - Ⓑ England
   - Ⓒ France
   - Ⓓ Ireland

3. Most of Stonehenge was probably built in the _____.
   - Ⓐ spring
   - Ⓑ summer
   - Ⓒ fall
   - Ⓓ winter

4. Archeologists think Stonehenge was built _____.
   - Ⓐ a few years ago
   - Ⓑ hundreds of years ago
   - Ⓒ thousands of years ago
   - Ⓓ millions of years ago

5. Stonehenge was probably not originally built for _____.
   - Ⓐ tourists
   - Ⓑ religious reasons
   - Ⓒ a burial ground
   - Ⓓ to tell the seasons

Bonus: On the back of this page, draw a picture of Stonehenge the way it may have looked thousands of years ago. Write a caption under the picture, telling an interesting fact about the monument.

England's Famous Monument

In southwestern England is a series of unusual rock formations. The rocks are called Stonehenge, which means "hanging stones." Here are sets of stones set up in a trilithon pattern. A trilithon is made of two stone pillars with a slab of rock laid across the top.

Hauling the Gigantic Stones

The largest rocks used to create Stonehenge were not from the area. The stones, which weighed up to 50 tons (45 metric tonnes) each, were dragged to the site from about 19 miles (30 km) away. People believe the rocks were hauled there in winter. The ground in winter in this area is usually full of ice and snow, making it easier to move the rocks.

Building the Monument

It is believed Stonehenge was constructed in three different stages. The first stage took place almost 5,000 years ago. A large circular earth wall was dug. The earth wall may have been used as a burial ground. A large stone was placed near the center of the circle. During the second stage, large blue stones were placed in the circle. Finally, in the third stage, up to 1,000 men hauled enormous sandstone rocks and placed them in an outer circle. The sandstone rocks were also called sarsen stones. Some of the sarsen stones were used to make five trilithon patterns. People are most amazed by the construction of the trilithons, some of which are still standing today.

The Meaning of Stonehenge

Why was the monument built? Some scientists think it's a burial ground. There are 400 burial sites nearby. Gold breastplates used in warfare have been found in the burial grounds. Others think Stonehenge was built by early astronomers. Scientists believe that when a person stands in the center of the monument, the changing of seasons can be seen. Many people think Stonehenge was built for religious ceremonies. A group of people called "Druids" have practiced their religion at Stonehenge for hundreds of years.

For whatever reason Stonehenge was built, it remains an amazing sight.

trilithon pattern

Nonfiction Reading Practice, Grade 5 • EMC 3316 • ©2003 by Evan-Moor Corp.

Name _____

England's Famous Monument

Fill in the bubble to answer each question or complete each sentence.

1. What does the word *Stonehenge* mean?
   - Ⓐ circular rocks
   - Ⓑ gigantic stones
   - Ⓒ hanging stones
   - Ⓓ burial ground

2. How many rocks are in a trilithon?
   - Ⓐ 3
   - Ⓑ 4
   - Ⓒ 6
   - Ⓓ 12

3. About _____ men were needed to lift the heavy stones.
   - Ⓐ 2
   - Ⓑ 10
   - Ⓒ 100
   - Ⓓ 1,000

4. Why do some people think Stonehenge was built by astronomers?
   - Ⓐ The rocks point toward the moon.
   - Ⓑ The passing of seasons can be seen there.
   - Ⓒ The sun always shines there.
   - Ⓓ Burial grounds are nearby.

5. What evidence is given to support the theory that Stonehenge was a burial ground?
   - Ⓐ It is constructed of trilithons.
   - Ⓑ People practiced their religion there.
   - Ⓒ There are 400 grave sites nearby.
   - Ⓓ King Arthur had it built for religious reasons.

Bonus: Stonehenge was probably built as a burial ground, for religious reasons, or to tell the passing of seasons. On the back of this page, write why you think Stonehenge was built thousands of years ago.

Building Stonehenge

On the plains of southwestern England stands an ancient monument called Stonehenge. Stonehenge consists of a group of gigantic rough-cut stones set in circles. How did ancient people construct this enormous monument without the use of modern tools?

Construction Site

Historians agree that Stonehenge was built in three phases. The first phase took place about 2800 B.C. At this time, a large circular earth wall was made. Historians believe the wall was dug with tools made from antlers of red deer. The shoulder blades of cattle were used as picks and shovels. When completed, the earth wall was about 320 feet (98 m) in diameter. A 16-foot (5-meter) tall stone was placed near the center.

Circle of Blue Stones

The second phase of Stonehenge started around 2150 B.C. About 60 large boulders, called blue stones, were placed inside the earthen wall. The blue stones, each weighing up to 4 tons (3.6 metric tonnes), came from the mountainous region of Wales. The stones were transported over water and land nearly 240 miles (384 km) to the site. Later, the blue stones were rearranged into horseshoe patterns.

Gigantic Sarsen Stones

Then around 2000 B.C., 30 enormous blocks of sandstone, called sarsen stones, were placed in an outer circle. A continuous circle of smaller stones stood on top of the larger sarsen stones. Each heavy sarsen stone weighed as much as 50 tons (45 metric tonnes). Almost 1,000 men were needed to drag each sarsen stone to the site from about 19 miles (30 km) away.

Hundreds of men were needed to raise a sarsen stone to a standing position.

Some sarsen stones were set up in a trilithon pattern. A trilithon consisted of two stone pillars with a horizontal stone, called a lintel, on top. Holes were dug for the two stone pillars. Teams of men used great levers and ropes to raise the pillars into an upright position. The stone lintel was laid across the pillars to complete the trilithon. Each of the five trilithons built stood up to 22 feet (7 m) tall. They were arranged in a horseshoe pattern within the inner circle.

Stonehenge was probably completed around 1500 B.C.

Nonfiction Reading Practice, Grade 5 • EMC 3316 • ©2003 by Evan-Moor Corp.

Name _____

Building Stonehenge

Fill in the bubble to answer each question or complete each sentence.

1. The first building stage of Stonehenge was _____.
   - Ⓐ a circular earth wall
   - Ⓑ a circle of blue stones
   - Ⓒ a trilithon
   - Ⓓ a gigantic sarsen stone

2. About how long ago did the construction of Stonehenge begin?
   - Ⓐ 1,000 years
   - Ⓑ 2,000 years
   - Ⓒ 5,000 years
   - Ⓓ 10,000 years

3. What were the largest stones at Stonehenge called?
   - Ⓐ blue stones
   - Ⓑ sarsen stones
   - Ⓒ trilithons
   - Ⓓ rough-cut stones

4. A trilithon uses how many stones?
   - Ⓐ 1
   - Ⓑ 2
   - Ⓒ 3
   - Ⓓ 5 or more

5. Why did large stones have to be brought to the construction site?
   - Ⓐ The large stones were scattered all over the Stonehenge area.
   - Ⓑ The Stonehenge area had only sarsen stones.
   - Ⓒ England did not have any stones.
   - Ⓓ There were no gigantic stones at the location of Stonehenge.

Bonus: On the back of this page, explain how men constructed the five trilithons.

Iroquois League of Nations

Introducing the Topic

1. Reproduce page 15 for individual students, or make a transparency to use with a group or the whole class.

2. Show students the map. Point out the five Native American tribes that lived in the area near Lake Ontario. Tell students these tribes shared a common language and similar customs, but the tribes didn't always get along. They competed for the same hunting and fishing grounds, and much fighting occurred between the tribes.

Reading the Selections

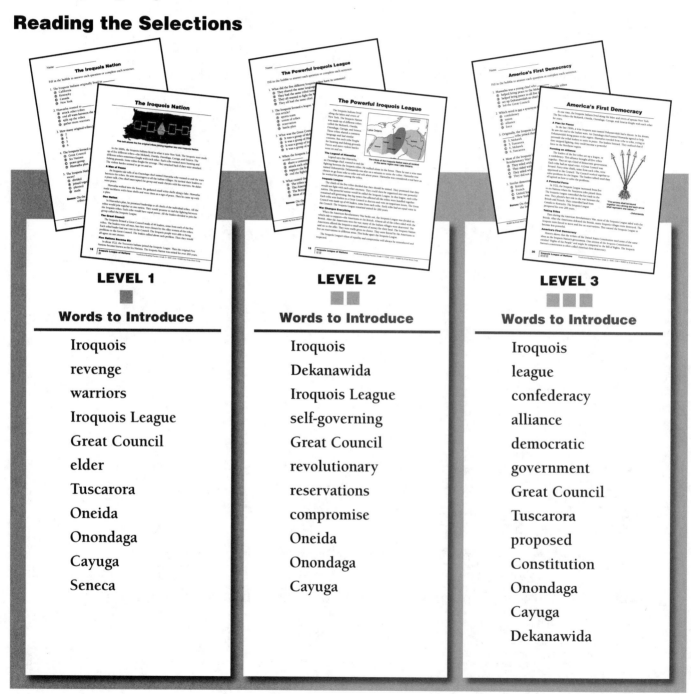

LEVEL 1
◼
Words to Introduce

Iroquois

revenge

warriors

Iroquois League

Great Council

elder

Tuscarora

Oneida

Onondaga

Cayuga

Seneca

LEVEL 2
◼◼
Words to Introduce

Iroquois

Dekanawida

Iroquois League

self-governing

Great Council

revolutionary

reservations

compromise

Oneida

Onondaga

Cayuga

LEVEL 3
◼◼◼
Words to Introduce

Iroquois

league

confederacy

alliance

democratic

government

Great Council

Tuscarora

proposed

Constitution

Onondaga

Cayuga

Dekanawida

The Iroquois Nation, 1600s

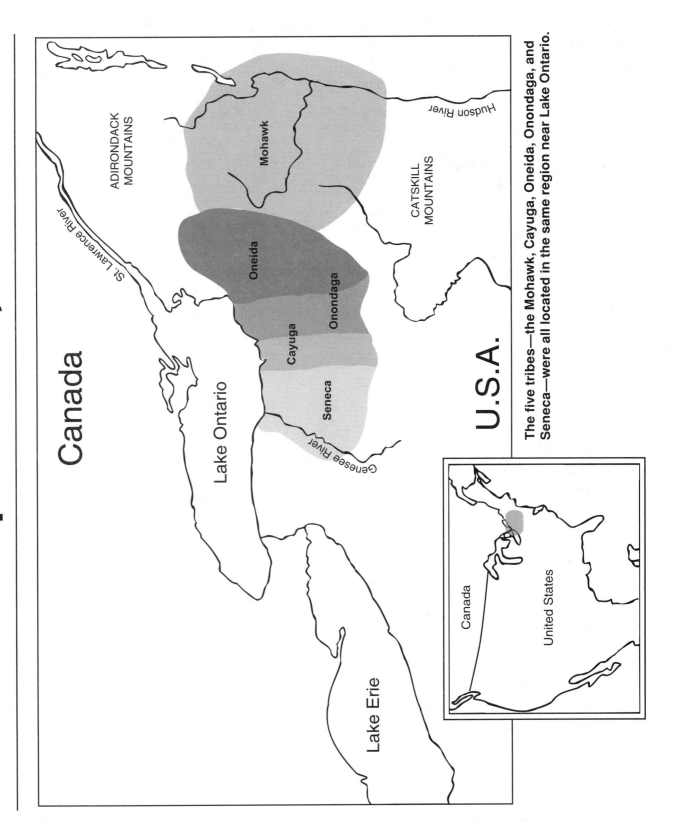

Canada

ADIRONDACK MOUNTAINS

St. Lawrence River

Lake Ontario

Lake Erie

Mohawk

Oneida

Cayuga

Onondaga

Seneca

Genesee River

CATSKILL MOUNTAINS

Hudson River

U.S.A.

The five tribes—the Mohawk, Cayuga, Oneida, Onondaga, and Seneca—were all located in the same region near Lake Ontario.

Canada

United States

The Iroquois Nation

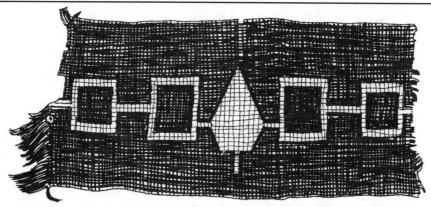

This belt shows the five original tribes joining together into one Iroquois Nation.

In the 1600s, the Iroquois Indians lived in what is now New York. The Iroquois were made up of five different tribes—the Mohawk, Oneida, Onondaga, Cayuga, and Seneca. The different tribes sometimes fought with each other. Each tribe wanted more hunting and fishing grounds. Some tribes fought for revenge. They attacked back if they were attacked. The violent battles seemed to go on and on.

A Man of Peace

An Iroquois tale tells of an Onondaga chief named Hiawatha who wanted to end the wars between the tribes. He sent messengers to all the Indian villages. He invited their leaders to a peace talk. One chief interrupted the group and made threats with his warriors. He didn't want peace.

Hiawatha walked into the forest. He gathered small white shells along a lake. Hiawatha made necklaces with these shells and wore them as a sign of peace. Then he came up with a plan.

One Nation

In Hiawatha's plan, he promised leadership to all chiefs of the individual tribes. All the tribes would join together as one nation. They would promise to end the fighting between the Iroquois tribes. Each tribe would have equal power. All the leaders decided to join the group called the Iroquois League.

The Great Council

The Iroquois formed a Great Council made of 49 leaders, some from each of the five tribes. The leaders were all men, but they were chosen by the elder women of the tribes. Each tribal leader had one vote in the Council. The Iroquois people were able to bring problems to the Great Council. The leaders talked about each problem. Then they would all agree on one answer.

Five Nations Become Six

In about 1722, the Tuscarora Indians joined the Iroquois League. Then the original Five Nations became known as the Six Nations. The Iroquois Nation was united for over 200 years.

Name _____

The Iroquois Nation

Fill in the bubble to answer each question or complete each sentence.

1. The Iroquois Indians originally lived in _____.
   - Ⓐ California
   - Ⓑ Kentucky
   - Ⓒ Canada
   - Ⓓ New York

2. Hiawatha wanted to _____.
   - Ⓐ attack other tribes
   - Ⓑ end all wars between the tribes
   - Ⓒ split up the tribes
   - Ⓓ gather more warriors

3. How many original tribes joined together to form the Iroquois League?
   - Ⓐ 2
   - Ⓑ 3
   - Ⓒ 5
   - Ⓓ 6

4. The Iroquois formed a _____ that helped resolve problems for the League.
   - Ⓐ Great Council
   - Ⓑ Six Nations
   - Ⓒ peace group
   - Ⓓ Hiawatha plan

5. The Iroquois Nation was united for 200 years. What does the word *united* mean?
   - Ⓐ divided
   - Ⓑ joined together
   - Ⓒ planned
   - Ⓓ made

Bonus: On the back of this page, write about what Hiawatha wanted for all the tribes of the Iroquois.

The Powerful Iroquois League

The Iroquois Indians lived along the lakes and rivers of New York. The Iroquois Nation was made up of different tribes called the Mohawk, Oneida, Onondaga, Cayuga, and Seneca. These tribes shared a common language and had similar customs. But each tribe fought for hunting and fishing grounds. Fierce and more violent battles went on and on.

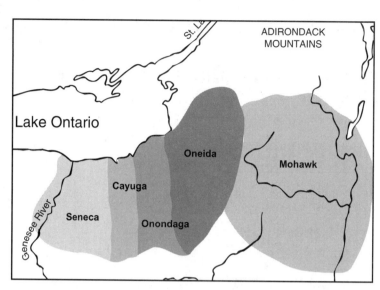

The tribes of the Iroquois Nation were all located in the same region near Lake Ontario.

The Legend of Hiawatha

Legend says that Hiawatha, an Onondaga chief, wanted to end the fighting between the Iroquois tribes. He walked alone in the forest. There he met a wise man named Dekanawida. Dekanawida was also on a mission to unite the tribes. Hiawatha was chosen to go from tribe to tribe and talk about peace. Hiawatha was considered a real hero as he worked for peace among the tribes.

Iroquois League

The chiefs of the five tribes decided that they should be united. They promised that they would not fight with each other anymore. They could then be organized into one powerful nation. The powerful nation would be called the Iroquois League. In this league, each tribe remained self-governing. But big issues that affected all the tribes were handled together. Each tribe sent leaders to a Great Council to discuss and vote on important issues. The Great Council was made up of 49 leaders, some from each tribe. Each tribe had an equal voice in the Council. The Iroquois League remained united for 200 years.

War Changes Everything

When the American Revolutionary War broke out, the Iroquois League was divided on which side to support—the Americans or the British. Almost all of the tribes sided with the British. After the Americans won the war, many of the Indian villages were destroyed. The Americans offered the Iroquois a small amount of money for their land. The Iroquois Nation said no to the offer. They were really given no choice. They were forced by the Americans to live on reservations in different areas. This broke apart the Iroquois League.

The Iroquois League's ideas of equality and compromise will always be remembered and respected.

The Powerful Iroquois League

Fill in the bubble to answer each question or complete each sentence.

1. What did the five different Iroquois tribes have in common?
   - Ⓐ They shared the same language.
   - Ⓑ They had the same tribal names.
   - Ⓒ They all wanted to fight the British.
   - Ⓓ They all had the same chief.

2. The Iroquois formed a league. What does the word *league* mean as used in this article?
   - Ⓐ sports team
   - Ⓑ union of tribes
   - Ⓒ reservation
   - Ⓓ battle plan

3. What was the Great Council?
   - Ⓐ It was a group of Mohawk leaders.
   - Ⓑ It was a group of Hiawatha's people.
   - Ⓒ It was a group of Iroquois leaders.
   - Ⓓ It was a group of warriors.

4. When the Iroquois League was formed, the leaders promised that they would _____.
   - Ⓐ share a common language
   - Ⓑ attack each other to gain hunting and fishing grounds
   - Ⓒ support the British in the American Revolutionary War
   - Ⓓ end the fighting between the tribes

5. What caused the breakup of the powerful Iroquois League?
   - Ⓐ The tribes started fighting each other.
   - Ⓑ The Americans won the war and forced the Iroquois onto reservations.
   - Ⓒ The British forced the Iroquois to fight with them in the war.
   - Ⓓ Most of the Iroquois leaders were killed in the war.

Bonus: On the back of this page, write how the results of the American Revolutionary War affected the Iroquois League.

America's First Democracy

At one time, the Iroquois Indians lived along the lakes and rivers of upstate New York. The five tribes—the Mohawk, Oneida, Onondaga, Cayuga, and Seneca—fought with each other for years.

A Plan for Peace

In the late 1500s, a wise Iroquois man named Dekanawida had a dream. In his dream, he saw the end to the Indian wars. An Onondaga chief named Hiawatha agreed to help Dekanawida bring peace to the region. Hiawatha traveled from tribe to tribe, trying to persuade the tribal leaders to unite in peace. The leaders listened. They realized that if they stopped fighting, they could become a powerful force in the Northeast region.

Forming an Alliance

The leaders of the five tribes set up a league, or a confederacy. This alliance brought all five tribes together. They set up a kind of democratic government. Each tribe had an equal voice. A Great Council was formed. Forty-nine chiefs, some from each tribe, were appointed to the Council. The Council worked together to solve problems for the league. The leaders talked until they all agreed on how to solve the problems.

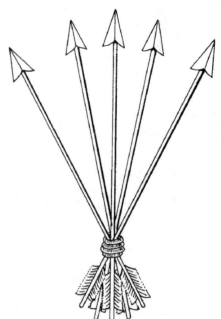

"Five arrows shall be bound together very strong and each arrow shall represent one nation..."

–Dekanawida

A Powerful Force

In 1722, the Iroquois League increased from five to six Nations when the Tuscarora tribe joined them. The Iroquois League controlled the fur trade in the area. They played a key role in the war between British and French. They controlled land from Canada to Kentucky. The Iroquois League prospered for over 200 years.

Taking Sides

Then during the American Revolutionary War, most of the Iroquois League sided with the British. After the Americans defeated the British, many Iroquois villages were destroyed. The Iroquois were forced to move and live on reservations. This caused the Iroquois League to become less powerful.

America's First Democracy

History shows that the writers of the United States Constitution used some of the same ideas as the Iroquois Nation's government. One section of the Iroquois Constitution is entitled "Rights of the People" and might be compared to the Bill of Rights. The Iroquois Nation's constitution is often called America's first democracy.

Name _____

America's First Democracy

Fill in the bubble to answer each question or complete each sentence.

1. Hiawatha was a young chief who _____.
   Ⓐ helped bring peace to the Mohawk and Oneida tribes
   Ⓑ helped bring peace to all five Iroquois tribes
   Ⓒ set up Dekanawida as chief of all the Iroquois
   Ⓓ led the Great Council

2. Which word is not a synonym for the word *league*?
   Ⓐ confederacy
   Ⓑ union
   Ⓒ alliance
   Ⓓ force

3. Originally, the Iroquois League was made up of _____ tribes until the _____ tribe joined them.
   Ⓐ 5, Mohawk
   Ⓑ 5, Tuscarora
   Ⓒ 6, Mohawk
   Ⓓ 6, Tuscarora

4. Most of the Iroquois League sided with which group during the American Revolutionary War?
   Ⓐ They sided with the British.
   Ⓑ They sided with the Americans.
   Ⓒ They sided with the Iroquois.
   Ⓓ They did not side with any group.

5. Similar democratic ideas appear in both the Iroquois and _____ constitutions.
   Ⓐ British
   Ⓑ French
   Ⓒ United States
   Ⓓ New York

Bonus: On the back of this page, write a paragraph explaining why you think the Iroquois League will always be remembered in history.

Shackleton's Antarctic Expedition

Introducing the Topic

1. Reproduce page 23 for individual students, or make a transparency to use with a group or the whole class.

2. Show students the map of Ernest Shackleton's 1914 attempted expedition to the South Pole. Share with students that another explorer, Roald Amundsen, was the first explorer to reach the pole in 1911. Shackleton's goal was to be the first to cross the polar ice cap. Explain that Shackleton's crew sailed from England to South Georgia Island. That is where the real story begins.

Reading the Selections

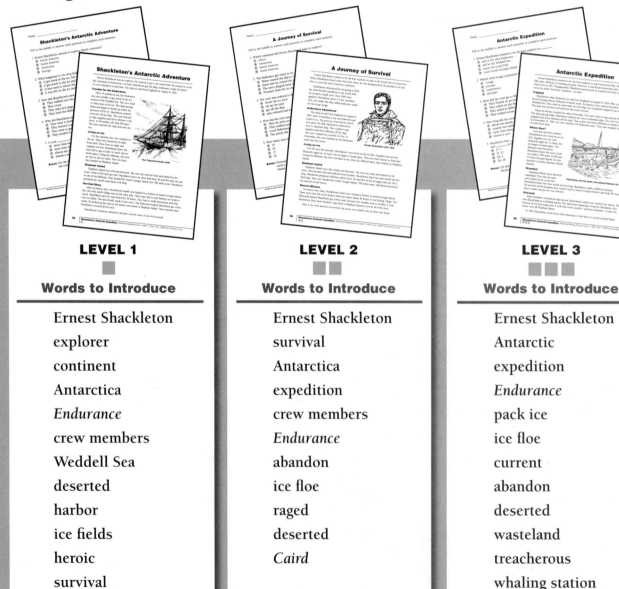

LEVEL 1	LEVEL 2	LEVEL 3
■	■ ■	■ ■ ■
Words to Introduce	**Words to Introduce**	**Words to Introduce**
Ernest Shackleton	Ernest Shackleton	Ernest Shackleton
explorer	survival	Antarctic
continent	Antarctica	expedition
Antarctica	expedition	*Endurance*
Endurance	crew members	pack ice
crew members	*Endurance*	ice floe
Weddell Sea	abandon	current
deserted	ice floe	abandon
harbor	raged	deserted
ice fields	deserted	wasteland
heroic	*Caird*	treacherous
survival		whaling station
		survival
		Roald Amundsen

Ernest Shackleton's
Antarctic Expedition, 1914

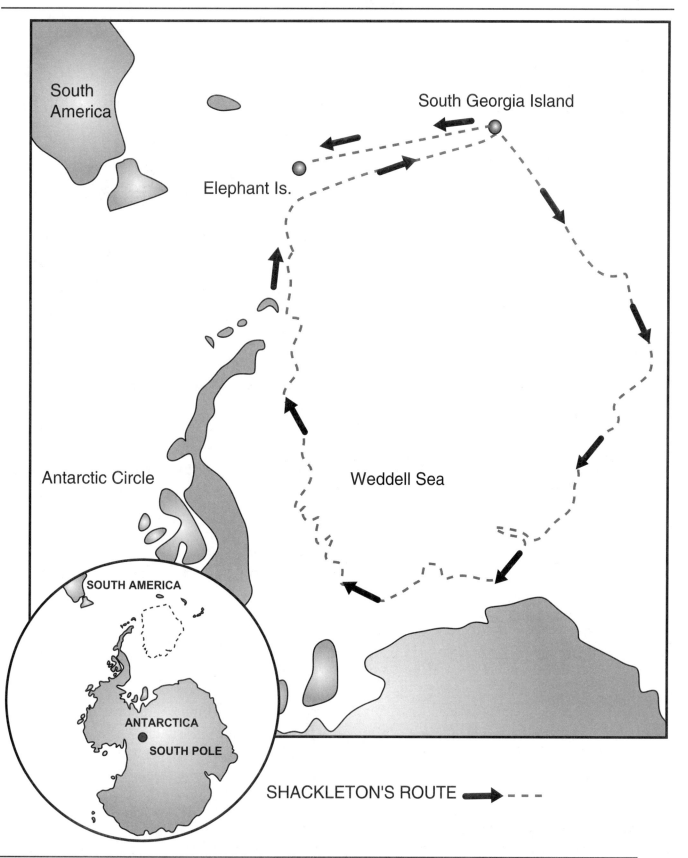

South America

South Georgia Island

Elephant Is.

Antarctic Circle

Weddell Sea

SOUTH AMERICA

ANTARCTICA

SOUTH POLE

SHACKLETON'S ROUTE

Shackleton's Antarctic Adventure

Ernest Shackleton was an explorer. He wanted to go to the South Pole. He wanted to cross the continent of Antarctica—on foot! Shackleton got his ship, *Endurance*, ready. He hired 27 crew members to join him. The ship set sail from England on August 8, 1914.

Trouble for the Endurance

After 14 months at sea, the *Endurance* ran into trouble. It got stuck in the icy waters of the Weddell Sea. The crew tried to chip away at the ice. The ship sprung leaks and began to break up under the pressure of the ice. Shackleton ordered everyone off the ship. The crew hurried to take supplies and three lifeboats with them. In November, the ship fell apart. The men watched the ship sink into the sea.

Living on Ice

For five months, the crew camped on the ice. They were hundreds of miles from land. Tents froze at night and supplies ran low. Shackleton knew the men had to get to land. In April, the ice broke apart. Using the lifeboats, the crew set sail on the icy water. After six days, they landed on Elephant Island.

The *Endurance* frozen solid

Elephant Island

Elephant Island was cold and deserted. The crew ate seals for food and melted ice for water. Some of the men got sick. Shackleton knew he must find help. He and five men set sail in one of the lifeboats. They headed for South Georgia Island over 700 miles away. Shackleton promised he would come back with help.

Survival Story

After seventeen days, Shackleton's small crew landed in a harbor on South Georgia Island. But, the only small village was on the other side. Three men had to stay behind, too weak to travel. Shackleton and two men hiked for 36 hours. They had to climb mountains and hike over ice fields. The men finally made it into town. The fishermen helped Shackleton get a boat ready. He picked up his men at the harbor and sailed to Elephant Island. Three months later, Shackleton rescued all the men.

Shackleton's Antarctic adventure became a heroic story of survival instead.

Name _____

Shackleton's Antarctic Adventure

Fill in the bubble to answer each question or complete each sentence.

1. Ernest Shackleton wanted to explore which continent?
   - Ⓐ North America
   - Ⓑ South America
   - Ⓒ Antarctica
   - Ⓓ Europe

2. What happened to the ship *Endurance*?
   - Ⓐ It got stuck in the ice, but was eventually saved.
   - Ⓑ It got stuck in the ice and eventually sunk.
   - Ⓒ It was used to rescue the crew.
   - Ⓓ It was left on the ice until spring.

3. How did Shackleton's crew get to Elephant Island?
   - Ⓐ They walked over the ice.
   - Ⓑ They swam.
   - Ⓒ They used sled dogs to carry them.
   - Ⓓ They used the lifeboats from the ship.

4. Why did Shackleton and five men leave Elephant Island?
   - Ⓐ They went to look for fresh food.
   - Ⓑ They wanted to go home.
   - Ⓒ They went to get help on another island.
   - Ⓓ They needed to repair the *Endurance*.

5. It took _____ to rescue the crew off Elephant Island.
   - Ⓐ more than two months
   - Ⓑ more than three months
   - Ⓒ almost six months
   - Ⓓ almost a year

Bonus: On the back of this page, write why Ernest Shackleton was a hero to his crew.

A Journey of Survival

Ernest Shackleton wanted to be the first explorer to sail to the South Pole of Antarctica. When Shackleton heard others beat him there, he was disappointed. He decided to be the first to cross the entire Antarctic continent.

Shackleton announced he was going to lead his third British expedition to the South Pole. He needed a small crew. Over 5,000 men applied! Shackleton chose 27 crew members. The crew made the ship called *Endurance* ready for the long voyage.

Ernest Shackleton 1874–1922

Endurance Abandoned

The ship set sail from England on August 8, 1914. After 14 months at sea, the *Endurance* got stuck in ice. The pressure from the ice slowly tore apart the ship. Shackleton ordered his crew to abandon ship. They rushed to get supplies and three lifeboats off the ship. The crew camped on a nearby ice floe. In November, the crew watched as the *Endurance* sank into the ocean.

Living on Ice

For the next five months, Shackleton's crew lived on the ice floe. Supplies ran out and blizzards raged on. In April, the ice began to break apart. This was their chance to find land. Using the lifeboats, the crew was back at sea. After six difficult days, they landed on Elephant Island.

Elephant Island

Elephant Island was cold, windy, and deserted. The crew ate seals and melted ice for water. Men became sick and suffered from frostbite. Shackleton knew his men would not last long. Shackleton prepared a lifeboat called *Caird*. He and five of the strongest men set off to find help. They were headed for South Georgia Island, 700 miles away. Shackleton promised his men he would return.

Rescue Mission

Seventeen days later, Shackelton's small crew reached a harbor at South Georgia Island. Three men were left at the harbor while the others hiked 36 hours to the fishing village. The fishermen helped Shackleton get a boat ready. Because the weather was so terrible, it took Shackleton three more months to get back to Elephant Island to rescue all of his men.

After a two-year journey of survival, the entire crew finally was on their way home.

Name _____

A Journey of Survival

Fill in the bubble to answer each question or complete each sentence.

1. Which continent did Ernest Shackleton want to explore?
   - Ⓐ Africa
   - Ⓑ Antarctica
   - Ⓒ North America
   - Ⓓ South America

2. The *Endurance* got stuck in ice. What caused the ship to break apart?
   - Ⓐ Water caused the ship to rust.
   - Ⓑ Snow and ice ruined the sails.
   - Ⓒ The men chipped away the ice and damaged the ship.
   - Ⓓ Pressure from the ice tore apart the ship.

3. The crew was ordered to abandon ship. What does the word *abandon* mean?
   - Ⓐ break the ice away
   - Ⓑ set up the sails
   - Ⓒ get off the ship
   - Ⓓ stay onboard and wait it out

4. How did the crew manage to survive on Elephant Island?
   - Ⓐ They ate seals and melted ice for water.
   - Ⓑ They walked around the island to keep warm.
   - Ⓒ Local fishermen gave them supplies.
   - Ⓓ The article did not say.

5. How many men survived the two-year journey?
   - Ⓐ 24
   - Ⓑ 26
   - Ⓒ 27
   - Ⓓ 28

Bonus: Pretend you were part of Shackleton's crew. On the back of this page, write a letter back home describing the horrible conditions on Elephant Island.

Antarctic Expedition

Ernest Shackleton wanted to be the first explorer to reach the South Pole. He came within 100 miles (160 km) of reaching his goal. However, it was Roald Amundsen who claimed the honor first in 1911. Disappointed, Shackleton announced he would be the first explorer to cross the entire Antarctic continent—on foot!

Trapped

Shackleton's ship *Endurance* set sail from England on August 8, 1914. After a stopover on South Georgia Island, *Endurance* headed south. In January, they entered the pack ice of the Weddell Sea. They tried to reach land, but the ship was completed trapped in an ice floe. The ship was carried northward by the ocean current.

Giant ice blocks crushed the sides of the ship. The crew tried to chip away at the ice. The ship sprung leaks. Shackleton ordered the crew to abandon ship. The crew hurried to get supplies and three lifeboats off the ship. They pulled the heavy lifeboats to thicker ice nearby. On November 21, 1915, the crew watched the *Endurance* sink. They were trapped hundreds of miles from land.

Where Now?

Over the next five months, Shackleton's crew lived on an ice floe. Supplies ran out, and blizzards raged on. In April, the ice began to break apart. The lifeboats were launched. Shackleton knew the crew could not make it 700 miles (1,120 km) to South Georgia Island. So they traveled to nearby Elephant Island instead.

Shackleton and his small crew aboard a lifeboat.

Stranded

Elephant Island was a deserted wasteland. The crew ate seals and sucked on ice to survive. Shackleton knew his crew would not last long. Shackleton made a difficult decision. He and five of his strongest men would travel to South Georgia Island to get help. He would have to leave twenty-two men behind.

Rescued

After seventeen treacherous days at sea, Shackleton's small crew reached the island. There they found help at a whaling station. The fishermen helped get a boat for Shackleton. But because of ice and rough seas, it took him three months—and four attempts—to save his entire crew off Elephant Island.

In 1919, Shackleton wrote about this amazing survival story in a book entitled *South*.

Shackleton's Antarctic Expedition Nonfiction Reading Practice, Grade 5 • EMC 3316 • ©2003 by Evan-Moor Corp.

Name _____

Antarctic Expedition

Fill in the bubble to answer each question or complete each sentence.

1. Ernest Shackleton wanted to be the first explorer to _____.
   - Ⓐ sail in the ship *Endurance*
   - Ⓑ sail in the Weddell Sea
   - Ⓒ reach the South Pole
   - Ⓓ reach South Georgia Island

2. Which of these is <u>not</u> a synonym for the word *expedition*?
   - Ⓐ voyage
   - Ⓑ journey
   - Ⓒ exploration
   - Ⓓ attempts

3. How did the crew get to Elephant Island?
   - Ⓐ They floated on an iceberg.
   - Ⓑ They sailed on the *Endurance*.
   - Ⓒ They sailed in lifeboats.
   - Ⓓ They walked across the ice.

4. How long did the crew have to wait on Elephant Island to be rescued?
   - Ⓐ about one month
   - Ⓑ exactly two months
   - Ⓒ more than three months
   - Ⓓ almost a year

5. Shackleton had _____ crew members at the beginning of the expedition and _____ at the end.
   - Ⓐ 27, 5
   - Ⓑ 27, 27
   - Ⓒ 28, 5
   - Ⓓ 28, 28

Bonus: On the back of this page, write what you think was the most difficult decision Shackleton had to make on this expedition.

The Battle of Little Bighorn

Introducing the Topic

1. Reproduce page 31 for individual students, or make a transparency to use with a group or the whole class.

2. Show students the map of where the Battle of Little Bighorn took place. Explain to students that in 1875, the United States wanted to buy the Black Hills from the Sioux Indians. The Sioux regarded this area as sacred. The Sioux told the United States government that the land could not be sold. Lieutenant Colonel George Custer was sent to force the Sioux off these lands and onto reservations. This led to a battle between the United States Army and the Sioux.

Reading the Selections

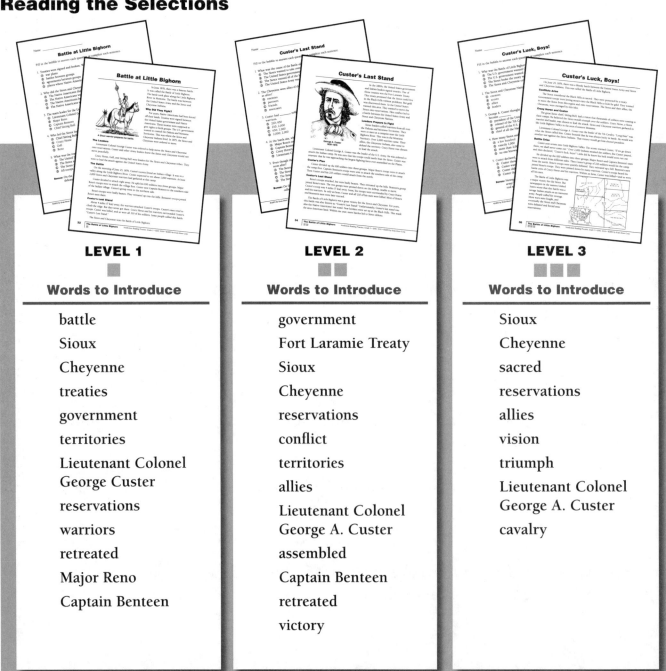

LEVEL 1

Words to Introduce

battle

Sioux

Cheyenne

treaties

government

territories

Lieutenant Colonel George Custer

reservations

warriors

retreated

Major Reno

Captain Benteen

LEVEL 2

Words to Introduce

government

Fort Laramie Treaty

Sioux

Cheyenne

reservations

conflict

territories

allies

Lieutenant Colonel George A. Custer

assembled

Captain Benteen

retreated

victory

LEVEL 3

Words to Introduce

Sioux

Cheyenne

sacred

reservations

allies

vision

triumph

Lieutenant Colonel George A. Custer

cavalry

The Battle of Little Bighorn

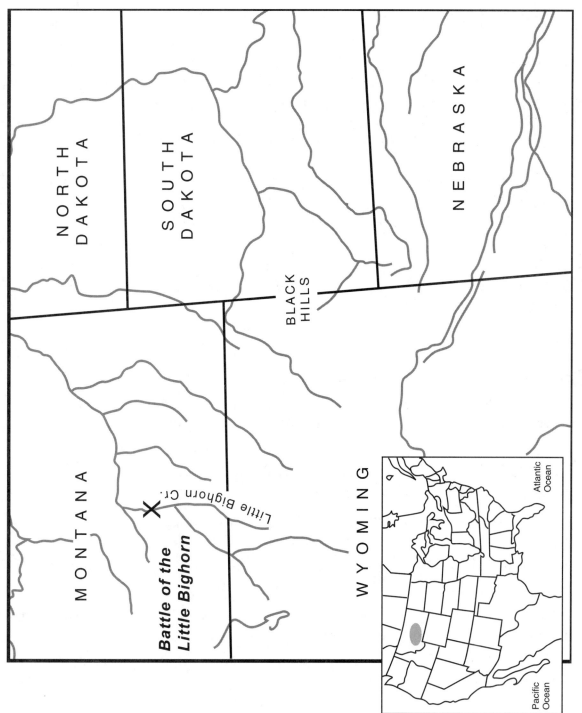

Between 1862 and 1877, the Sioux forcefully resisted the United States advance onto their lands. In 1876, in eastern Montana near the Little Bighorn River, the Sioux and their allies, the Cheyenne, fought the U.S. Army. The battle was called the Battle of Little Bighorn. It was the biggest victory for the Native Americans against the U.S. Army.

Battle at Little Bighorn

A Sioux warrior prepares for battle.

In June 1876, there was a famous battle. It was called the Battle of Little Bighorn. The battle took place along the Little Bighorn River in Montana. The battle was between the United States Army and the Sioux and Cheyenne Indians.

Why Did They Fight?

For years, Native Americans had been forced off their lands. Treaties were signed between the United States government and Native Americans. These treaties were supposed to give rights to both groups. The U.S. government wanted to control the Dakota and Montana Territories. This was where the Sioux and Cheyenne Indians lived. In 1875, the Sioux and Cheyenne were ordered to move.

The Leaders

Lieutenant Colonel George Custer was ordered to help move the Sioux and Cheyenne onto reservations. Custer and other Army leaders knew the Sioux and Cheyenne would not move peacefully.

Crazy Horse, Gall, and Sitting Bull were leaders for the Sioux and Cheyenne tribes. Crazy Horse was to lead the attack against the United States Army.

The Battle

On the morning of June 25, 1876, Custer's scouts found an Indian village. It was in a valley along the Little Bighorn River. Custer expected to see about 1,000 warriors. At least 2,000 Sioux and Cheyenne warriors had gathered at this camp.

Custer decided to attack right away. He split his 650 soldiers into three groups. Major Reno's troops were to attack the village first. Custer sent Captain Benteen to the southern side of the Indian village. Custer's group went to the northern side.

Reno's troops were badly beaten. They retreated up into the hills. Benteen's troops joined Reno's men there.

Custer's Last Stand

About 4 miles (7 km) away, the warriors attacked Custer's troops. Custer's men tried to climb the ridge. But they never got there. Crazy Horse and his warriors surrounded Custer's troops. Custer was killed, and so were all 210 of his soldiers. Some people called this battle "Custer's Last Stand."

The Sioux and Cheyenne won the Battle of Little Bighorn.

Name _____

Battle at Little Bighorn

Fill in the bubble to answer each question or complete each sentence.

1. Treaties were signed and broken. What are *treaties*?
   - Ⓐ war plans
   - Ⓑ battles between groups
   - Ⓒ agreements between groups
   - Ⓓ places where Native Americans lived

2. Why did the Sioux and Cheyenne battle with the United States Army?
   - Ⓐ The Native Americans did not want to share the land.
   - Ⓑ The Native Americans were warlike people.
   - Ⓒ The Native Americans broke the treaty.
   - Ⓓ The Native Americans were being forced off their lands.

3. The main leader of the United States Army was _____.
   - Ⓐ Lieutenant Colonel George Custer
   - Ⓑ Major Reno
   - Ⓒ Captain Benteen
   - Ⓓ Chief Sitting Bull

4. Who led the Sioux Indian attack against Custer?
   - Ⓐ Chief Sitting Bull
   - Ⓑ Crazy Horse
   - Ⓒ Gall
   - Ⓓ Reno

5. What was the result of the Battle of Little Bighorn?
   - Ⓐ The United States Army won the battle.
   - Ⓑ The Sioux and Cheyenne won the battle.
   - Ⓒ The Sioux won, but the Cheyenne lost.
   - Ⓓ All troops of the United States Army were killed.

Bonus: On the back of this page, write why you think the Sioux and Cheyenne defeated Custer's troops.

Custer's Last Stand

George A. Custer
1839–1876

In the 1800s, the United States government and Indian leaders signed treaties. One of those treaties was the Fort Laramie Treaty. This treaty promised that the Sioux could live in the Black Hills without problems. But gold was discovered there. So the United States wanted this area. They wanted to move the Sioux onto reservations. This conflict led to a battle between the United States Army and the Sioux and Cheyenne Nations.

Leaders Prepare to Fight

Sioux leaders called warriors from all over the Dakota and Montana Territories. They were to meet at a campsite near the Little Bighorn River. This was in the Montana Territory. Over 2,000 warriors came. Their allies, the Cheyenne Indians, also came to defend the territory. Crazy Horse was chosen to lead the attack.

Lieutenant Colonel George A. Custer was the leader of the U.S. Army. He was ordered to attack the Indian camp. He was sure that his troops could easily beat the Sioux. Custer was unaware that he was approaching the largest fighting force ever assembled on the Plains.

Custer's Plan

Custer divided the 650 soldiers into three groups. Major Reno's troops were to attack the camp first. Captain Benteen's troops were sent to attack the southern side of the camp. Then Custer and his 210 soldiers would attack from the north.

Custer's Last Stand

Reno's troops attacked, but were badly beaten. They retreated up the hills. Benteen's group joined Reno's men. The two groups were pinned down on the hilltop, unable to move. Custer's troop was 4 miles (7 km) away. Soon, his troops were surrounded by Crazy Horse and his warriors. In only an hour, Custer and all 210 of his men were killed. Most of Reno's and Benteen's men were later rescued.

The Battle of Little Bighorn was a great victory for the Sioux and Cheyenne. For years, this battle was also known as "Custer's Last Stand." Unfortunately, Custer's last stand was also the Native Americans' last stand. New borders were set up in the Black Hills. This made the area American land. Within one year, more battles led to Sioux defeats.

Name _____

Custer's Last Stand

Fill in the bubble to answer each question or complete each sentence.

1. What was the cause of the Battle of Little Bighorn?
   Ⓐ The Sioux wanted to take over United States government lands.
   Ⓑ The United States government wanted to take over Sioux lands.
   Ⓒ The Sioux wanted all of the Montana Territory.
   Ⓓ The United States Army wanted to win more battles.

2. The Cheyenne were allies of the Sioux. Which word does not mean the same as *allies*?
   Ⓐ enemies
   Ⓑ partners
   Ⓒ friends
   Ⓓ associates

3. Custer had _____ soldiers and the Native Americans had over _____ warriors.
   Ⓐ 210; 650
   Ⓑ 210; 2,000
   Ⓒ 650; 2,000
   Ⓓ 2,000; 2,000

4. At the battle site, what happened in only one hour?
   Ⓐ Major Reno's troops were killed.
   Ⓑ Captain Benteen's troops retreated.
   Ⓒ Crazy Horse's warriors fled to the hills.
   Ⓓ Lieutenant Colonel Custer and his troops were killed.

5. Even though the battle was a great victory for the Sioux, what happened soon after?
   Ⓐ The Sioux gave the Black Hills to new settlers.
   Ⓑ The Sioux lived peacefully on their lands.
   Ⓒ The Sioux were defeated.
   Ⓓ The Sioux won many more battles.

Bonus: On the back of this page, write why the Battle of Little Bighorn was also called "Custer's Last Stand."

Custer's Luck, Boys!

On June 25, 1876, there was a bloody battle between the United States Army and Sioux and Cheyenne Indians. This was called the Battle of Little Bighorn.

Conflicts Arise

The Sioux considered the Black Hills as sacred. They were protected by a treaty. Government troops were letting miners into the Black Hills to look for gold. They wanted to move the Sioux from this region and onto reservations. The Sioux and their allies, the Cheyenne, were outraged by this idea.

Crazy Horse and Custer

The great Sioux chief, Sitting Bull, had a vision that thousands of soldiers were coming to their camps. He believed the Sioux would triumph over the soldiers. Crazy Horse, a Sioux warrior and leader, was chosen to lead the attack. Sioux and Cheyenne warriors gathered in the Little Bighorn Valley in the area of eastern Montana.

Lieutenant Colonel George A. Custer was the leader of the 7th Cavalry. "Long Hair" was what the Sioux called him. Custer boasted that he was always lucky in battle. He would win another war against the Sioux Indians. That victory would get him elected president.

Battle Cries

Custer sent scouts into Little Bighorn Valley. The scouts warned Custer, "If we go down there, we shall never come out." Over 2,000 Indians awaited the soldiers. But Custer prayed, and then declared, "Custer's luck, boys!" Little did he know his luck would soon run out.

He divided the 650 soldiers into three groups. Major Reno's and Captain Benteen's men were to attack from different sides. Then Custer's group of 210 soldiers would hit the camp from the north. Reno's troops were quickly defeated. They retreated up a hill. Benteen's men joined Reno's troops. They were pinned down by many warriors. Custer's troops heard the battle cries of Crazy Horse and his warriors. Within an hour, Custer was killed—and so were all his men.

The Battle of Little Bighorn was a major victory for the Sioux. But newspapers in the eastern United States wrote that this battle was a savage Indian attack on an innocent army. People called for revenge. More wars were fought, and eventually the Sioux and Cheyenne were defeated and forced onto reservations.

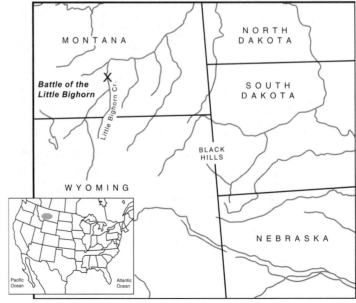

Name _____

Custer's Luck, Boys!

Fill in the bubble to answer each question or complete each sentence.

1. Why was the Battle of Little Bighorn fought?
   - Ⓐ The U.S. government wanted the Sioux to live in Montana.
   - Ⓑ The U.S. government wanted to move the Sioux from their lands.
   - Ⓒ The Sioux broke the treaty with the U.S. government.
   - Ⓓ The Sioux and Cheyenne could not get along.

2. The Sioux and Cheyenne Nations were _____.
   - Ⓐ enemies
   - Ⓑ scouts
   - Ⓒ allies
   - Ⓓ leaders

3. George A. Custer thought he could easily defeat the Sioux and then become _____.
   - Ⓐ president of the United States
   - Ⓑ colonel of the 7th Calvary
   - Ⓒ general of the U.S. Army
   - Ⓓ chief of all the Native Americans

4. How many Sioux and Cheyenne Indians were waiting for the U.S. Army?
   - Ⓐ a few hundred
   - Ⓑ exactly 1,000
   - Ⓒ more than 2,000
   - Ⓓ no one knows

5. Custer declared, "Custer's luck, boys!" What did he mean by this statement?
   - Ⓐ Custer thought it would take a lot of luck to win.
   - Ⓑ Custer wanted the soldiers to wish him luck.
   - Ⓒ Custer did not think he was very lucky in battle.
   - Ⓓ Custer thought he was lucky and would easily win the battle.

Bonus: Newspaper articles said the Indians led a "savage attack on an innocent army." On the back of this page, write a newspaper article telling the real story of what happened at the Battle of Little Bighorn.

The Ring of Fire

Introducing the Topic

1. Reproduce page 39 for individual students, or make a transparency to use with a group or the whole class.

2. Show students the map of the Ring of Fire. Tell students this is an area or zone along the edge of the Pacific Ocean that has many earthquakes and volcanoes. Point out the continents that are in this area. Discuss how close or far away students live from this area.

Reading the Selections

LEVEL 1
■

Words to Introduce

Philippines

zone

earthquakes

volcanoes

faults

San Andreas Fault

Indonesia

Mt. Pinatubo

Kilauea

LEVEL 2
■ ■

Words to Introduce

volcanoes

earthquakes

surface

slabs

plates

collide

faults

Richter scale

San Andreas Fault

magma

Kilauea

tsunami

shock wave

Indonesia

Krakatoa

LEVEL 3
■ ■ ■

Words to Introduce

zone

theory

plate tectonics

subduction

tectonic plates

faults

San Andreas Fault

magma

Kilauea

The Ring of Fire

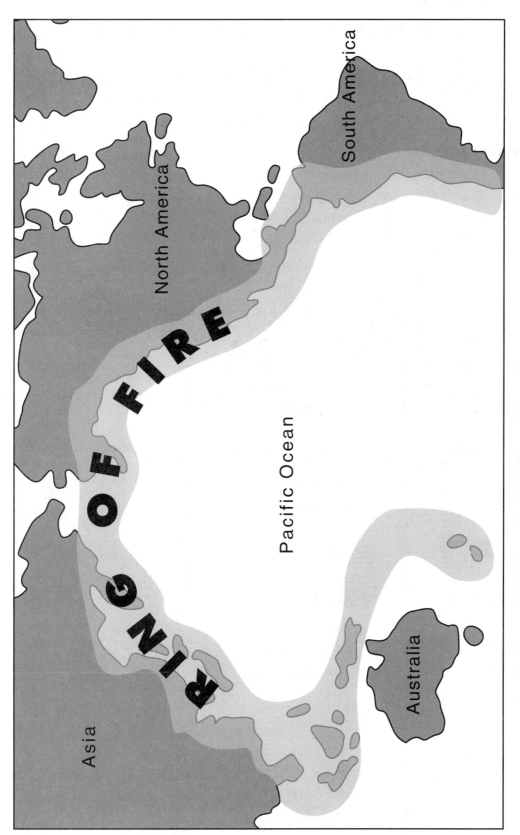

Asia

North America

South America

Australia

RING OF FIRE

Pacific Ocean

Do you live near the Ring of Fire? The Ring of Fire refers to a zone along the edge of the Pacific Ocean. This is where many earthquakes and volcanoes are located. The Ring of Fire stretches about 25,000 miles (40,000 km) from New Zealand northwest to the Philippines; northeast to Japan; east to Alaska; and south to Mexico, and the Andes Mountains of South America.

The Pacific Ring of Fire

You are on a sailing trip. You sail from New Zealand to the Philippines to Japan. From Japan, you sail to Alaska. From Alaska, you sail down the west coasts of North and South America. You just sailed an area called the Ring of Fire. This is a zone along the edge of the Pacific Ocean. It is where most of the world's volcanoes are located. It is where most earthquakes happen, too.

Plates on the Earth

The surface of Earth is made of plates. The plates are like giant rafts. They move just a few inches a year. The plates bump into each other. When they do this, one plate sinks beneath the other. This causes movement, which creates earthquakes. Volcanoes also happen when magma breaks through cracks in these plates.

Earthquakes

More than a million earthquakes a year shake the Earth. Each year, thousands of earthquakes happen along faults in the Ring of Fire area. Faults are breaks in the Earth's crust. They occur in weak areas of the Earth's rocks. A famous example is the San Andreas Fault in California. This fault is 700 miles (1,120 km) long. There have been several large earthquakes along this fault.

Volcanoes

There are about 1,500 active volcanoes on Earth. Over half of those occur along the Ring of Fire. Japan has more than 70 of them. Indonesia has 60 active volcanoes. Mt. Pinatubo in the Philippines is one of 30 in that country. Mt. St. Helens in Washington and Kilauea in Hawaii are America's most active volcanoes.

Volcanoes can destroy and then create new lands. Earthquakes also reshape land areas. The volcanoes and earthquakes along the Ring of Fire are constantly changing the Earth.

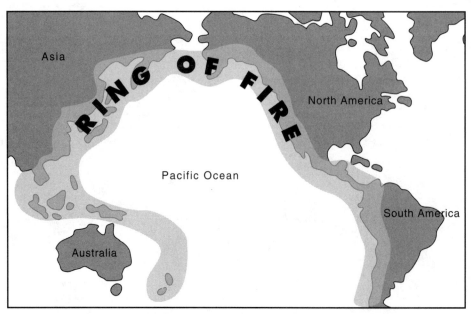

The Ring of Fire is about 25,000 miles (40,000 km) long.

Name _____

The Pacific Ring of Fire

Fill in the bubble to answer each question or complete each sentence.

1. The Ring of Fire is located along the edge of the _____.
   - Ⓐ Atlantic Ocean
   - Ⓑ Arctic Ocean
   - Ⓒ Pacific Ocean
   - Ⓓ Indian Ocean

2. What natural events happen along the Ring of Fire?
   - Ⓐ volcanoes
   - Ⓑ earthquakes
   - Ⓒ tornadoes
   - Ⓓ both volcanoes and earthquakes

3. What causes earthquakes?
   - Ⓐ Earth's plates bump into each other.
   - Ⓑ Magma breaks through the Earth's crust.
   - Ⓒ Violent shaking occurs in the ground.
   - Ⓓ Rocks fall to the ground.

4. About how many earthquakes happen each year along the Ring of Fire?
   - Ⓐ a few
   - Ⓑ hundreds
   - Ⓒ thousands
   - Ⓓ more than one million

5. What two volcanoes are active in the United States?
   - Ⓐ Mt. Pinatubo and Mt. St. Helens
   - Ⓑ Mt. St. Helens and Kilauea
   - Ⓒ San Andreas and Kilauea
   - Ⓓ There are no active volcanoes in the United States.

Bonus: On the back of this page, write about what happens along the Ring of Fire.

Along the Ring of Fire

The Ring of Fire is a long stretch of area along the rim of the Pacific Ocean. It is 25,000 miles (40,000 km) long. The Ring of Fire is where most of the world's volcanoes and earthquakes are located.

Plates on the Earth

The Earth's surface is broken into huge slabs of rock called plates. The plates are like giant rafts. These plates are in constant slow motion. Sometimes, the plates collide or push past each other. The edge of one heavier plate sinks beneath the other lighter plate. This causes movement. Movements of plates cause faults, or large breaks, in Earth's crust. Earthquakes happen along those faults. Volcanoes also happen when magma breaks through cracks in the plates.

Earthquakes

Every year, more than a million earthquakes shake the Earth. Eighty percent of the earthquakes happen along the Ring of Fire belt. Some earthquakes are too small to feel. The largest earthquake ever was in 1960 on the coast of Chile. It measured 9.5 on the Richter scale. California's San Andreas Fault has thousands of smaller earthquakes each year.

Volcanoes

There are about 1,500 active volcanoes on Earth. About half of those occur along the Ring of Fire. Japan has more than 70 of them. Mount St. Helens in the state of Washington is one. It erupted in 1980 and tore 1,300 feet (400 m) off the top of the mountain. Kilauea, on the island of Hawaii, has been erupting since 1983. Lava pours into the Pacific Ocean. The lava cools and hardens into rock, making the island grow in size.

Tsunamis

Tsunamis are giant waves that can travel thousands of miles. After an earthquake or a volcano erupts, a shock wave can ripple into the nearby ocean. This is what starts the tsunami moving. They can travel up to 500 miles per hour! As they get closer to shore, they slow down and get taller. The biggest tsunami in history came after Indonesia's Krakatoa volcano erupted in 1883. Thirty-six thousand people died from this giant wave.

Along the Ring of Fire, earthquakes, volcanoes, and tsunamis are constantly changing the Earth.

The lava flows from Kilauea are helping to increase the size of Hawaii.

Nonfiction Reading Practice, Grade 5 • EMC 3316 • ©2003 by Evan-Moor Corp.

Name _____

Along the Ring of Fire

Fill in the bubble to answer each question or complete each sentence.

1. The Ring of Fire is _____.
   - Ⓐ the surface of the earth
   - Ⓑ broken slabs of rock called plates
   - Ⓒ a large area along the rim of the Pacific Ocean
   - Ⓓ where all earthquakes and volcanoes occur

2. Along what ocean is the Ring of Fire located?
   - Ⓐ Atlantic Ocean
   - Ⓑ Pacific Ocean
   - Ⓒ Indian Ocean
   - Ⓓ Arctic Ocean

3. What natural events occur along the Ring of Fire?
   - Ⓐ only earthquakes
   - Ⓑ a few volcanoes
   - Ⓒ only tsunamis
   - Ⓓ many earthquakes, volcanoes, and tsunamis

4. What causes the Ring of Fire's earthquakes and volcanoes?
   - Ⓐ Earth's plates bump into each other.
   - Ⓑ Earth's plates get heavy.
   - Ⓒ Earth's plates get too light.
   - Ⓓ Earth's plates move too slowly.

5. What are tsunamis?
   - Ⓐ volcanoes
   - Ⓑ earthquakes
   - Ⓒ new volcanic islands
   - Ⓓ giant waves

Bonus: On the back of this page, write which natural event—an earthquake, a volcano, or a tsunami—you think would cause the most damage to an area along the Ring of Fire. Remember to include reasons why you think this way.

The Ring of Fire and Plate Tectonics

In the 1960s, scientists studied the area known as the Ring of Fire. The Ring of Fire is a horseshoe-shaped zone that stretches along the rim of the Pacific Ocean. It is 25,000 miles (40,000 km) long. Even though this seems like a large area, it is only about one percent of the Earth's surface. So why do half the world's active volcanoes and eighty percent of the earthquakes occur in this zone? Scientists developed a theory. It is called plate tectonics.

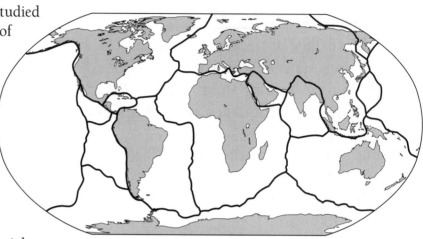

Earth's crust is made up of solid sections of rock called tectonic plates.

Plate Tectonics

The Earth's crust is not formed in one huge piece. It is divided into large sections of rock called tectonic plates. Tectonic plates are like giant rafts drifting in slow motion. They move just a few inches a year. The Earth's plates bump into each other. When they do this, one of the plates sinks beneath the other plate. This is called the process of subduction. The grinding movements of subduction cause many earthquakes and volcanoes to occur. Earthquakes and volcanoes occur on the edges of the tectonic plates. The Ring of Fire area is surrounded by many tectonic plates.

Earthquakes

Over a million earthquakes a year rattle the Earth. Thousands of the earthquakes happen along tectonic plates in the Ring of Fire. Where the tectonic plates meet, there are large faults, or breaks, in the Earth's crust. Faults are where most earthquakes occur. For example, the San Andreas Fault in California is 650 miles (1,040 km) long. It is a common place for earthquakes.

Volcanoes

Half of the 1,500 active volcanoes occur along the Ring of Fire. Volcanoes happen when magma breaks through weak areas or cracks in the tectonic plates. This can happen violently in an explosion. Or it can happen more slowly, causing lava to pour out of the volcano. Mount St. Helens in the state of Washington erupted violently in 1980. The volcano Kilauea, on the island of Hawaii, has been erupting since 1983. Lava slowly runs into the ocean, where it cools and hardens into rock.

Scientists now know that the constant motion of the tectonic plates along the Pacific Rim causes numerous earthquakes and volcanoes to occur.

Name _____

The Ring of Fire and Plate Tectonics

Fill in the bubble to answer each question or complete each sentence.

1. What are tectonic plates?
   Ⓐ magma beneath the Earth's surface
   Ⓑ giant waves
   Ⓒ rafts floating on the ocean
   Ⓓ huge slabs of rock on the Earth's surface

2. The edge of one plate sinking beneath the edge of another plate is a process called _____.
   Ⓐ tectonics
   Ⓑ subduction
   Ⓒ faults
   Ⓓ eruption

3. An earthquake occurs along a fault. What is a fault?
   Ⓐ a break in the Earth's crust
   Ⓑ a giant raft
   Ⓒ the grinding movements of the plates
   Ⓓ lava pouring into the ocean

4. Where do most of the world's volcanoes occur?
   Ⓐ New Zealand
   Ⓑ North America
   Ⓒ the Philippines
   Ⓓ along the Ring of Fire

5. Where do most earthquakes and volcanoes happen in the Ring of Fire?
   Ⓐ in the middle of the Pacific Ocean
   Ⓑ in the northern part of the zone
   Ⓒ along the edges of the tectonic plates
   Ⓓ along the coast of California

Bonus: Pretend you are a scientist giving a lecture about plate tectonics. On the back of this page, write a short speech explaining the theory of plate tectonics and how it affects the Ring of Fire area.

Magnetism

Introducing the Topic

1. Reproduce page 47 for individual students, or make a transparency to use with a group or the whole class.

2. Show the examples of common permanent magnets and discuss where these magnets are found in everyday life. Then show the students the electromagnet. Tell students that these kinds of temporary magnets are found in electric motors and other machines. Show the third example and talk about how magnets either attract or repel objects. The fourth example shows a magnetic field.

Reading the Selections

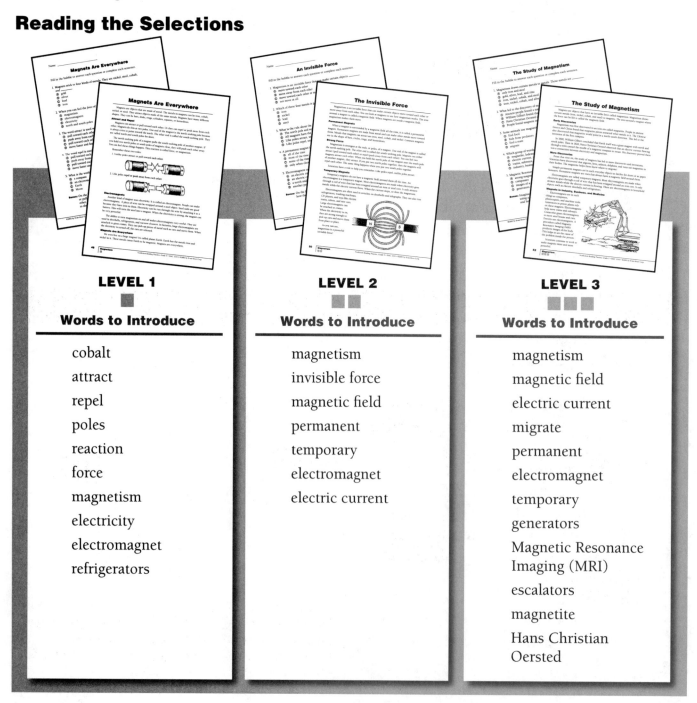

LEVEL 1

Words to Introduce

cobalt

attract

repel

poles

reaction

force

magnetism

electricity

electromagnet

refrigerators

LEVEL 2

Words to Introduce

magnetism

invisible force

magnetic field

permanent

temporary

electromagnet

electric current

LEVEL 3

Words to Introduce

magnetism

magnetic field

electric current

migrate

permanent

electromagnet

temporary

generators

Magnetic Resonance Imaging (MRI)

escalators

magnetite

Hans Christian Oersted

Magnetism

Common Permanent Magnets

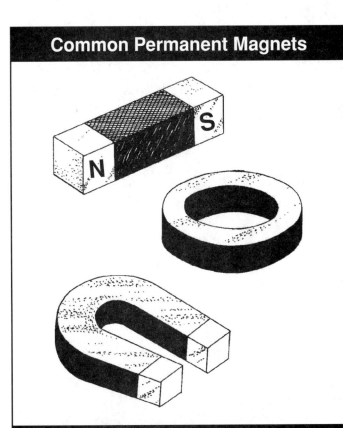

Electromagnet

An electromagnet is made when electricity goes through a coil of wire that has been wrapped around an iron or steel core.

The Power of Magnetism

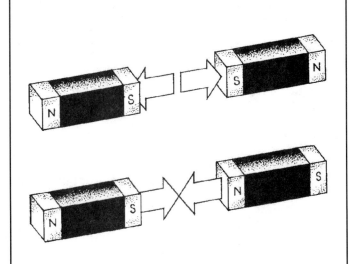

Unlike poles attract or pull toward each other.

Magnetic Field

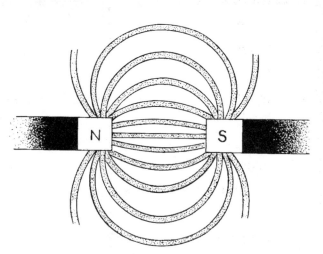

A magnetic field is shown as imaginary lines. The lines flow out of the north pole and into the south pole. The magnetic field of a bar magnet is strongest near the magnet's poles. That is where the lines lie closest to each other.

Magnets Are Everywhere

Magnets are objects that are made of metal. The metals in magnets can be iron, cobalt, nickel, or steel. They attract objects made of the same metals. Magnets have many different shapes. They can be bars, disks, rings, cylinders, squares, or horseshoes.

Attract and Repel

Magnets can attract or pull toward each other. Or they can repel or push away from each other. Magnets do this at two poles. One end of the magnet is the north-seeking pole because it always tries to point toward the north. The other end is called the south-seeking pole. They are called north and south poles for short.

The north-seeking pole of a magnet pulls the south-seeking pole of another magnet. If you hold two north poles or south poles of magnets close, they will push each other away. You can feel these things happen. This reaction is called force, or magnetism.

Remember these two rules:

1. Unlike poles attract or pull toward each other.

2. Like poles repel or push away from each other.

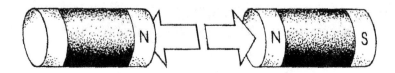

Electromagnets

Another kind of magnet uses electricity. It is called an electromagnet. People can make electromagnets. A piece of wire can be wrapped around a steel object. Steel nails are good because they have iron in them. Electricity can be run through the wire by attaching it to a battery. This will turn the steel into a magnet. When the electricity is strong, the magnet can be very powerful.

The ability to turn magnetism on and off makes electromagnets very useful. They are used in doorbells, refrigerators, and vacuum cleaners. In factories, huge electromagnets are attached to giant cranes. They can pick up pieces of metal such as cars and move them. When the electricity is turned off, the cars are released.

Magnets Are Everywhere

We even live on a huge magnet! It's called planet Earth. Earth has the metals iron and nickel in it. These metals cause Earth to be magnetic. Magnets are everywhere.

Nonfiction Reading Practice, Grade 5 • EMC 3316 • ©2003 by Evan-Moor Corp.

Name _____

Magnets Are Everywhere

Fill in the bubble to answer each question or complete each sentence.

1. Magnets stick to four kinds of metals. They are nickel, steel, cobalt, and _____.
   - Ⓐ gold
   - Ⓑ silver
   - Ⓒ lead
   - Ⓓ iron

2. When you can feel the force of magnets, this is called _____.
   - Ⓐ electricity
   - Ⓑ electromagnets
   - Ⓒ magnetism
   - Ⓓ north and south poles

3. The word attract is used when two magnets _____.
   - Ⓐ pull toward each other
   - Ⓑ push away from each other
   - Ⓒ pull toward each other and then push away
   - Ⓓ move faster and faster

4. The word repel is used when two magnets _____.
   - Ⓐ pull toward each other
   - Ⓑ push away from each other
   - Ⓒ pull toward each other and then push away
   - Ⓓ move faster and faster

5. What is the world's largest magnet?
   - Ⓐ a compass
   - Ⓑ an electromagnet
   - Ⓒ the Earth
   - Ⓓ the moon

Bonus: On the back of this page, write these two rules: 1. Unlike poles attract or pull toward each other. 2. Like poles repel or push away from each other. Draw labeled pictures of bar magnets under each of these rules to show what they mean.

An Invisible Force

Magnetism is an invisible force that can make certain objects move toward each other or move away from each other. You can look at magnets to see how magnetism works. The area around a magnet is called a magnetic field. When magnets are inside a magnetic field, magnetism makes them move.

Permanent Magnets

When a magnet is surrounded by a magnetic field all the time, it is called a permanent magnet. Permanent magnets are made from metal and can make other metals move toward them. Metals that magnets can attract are iron, steel, cobalt, and nickel. Common magnets are in the shape of bars, circles, rings, and horseshoes.

Strong Force

Magnetism is strongest at the ends, or poles, of a magnet. One end of the magnet is called the north-seeking pole. The other end is called the south-seeking pole. Magnets can either attract (pull toward each other) or repel (push away from each other). You can feel two magnets attract each other. When you hold the north pole of one magnet near the south pole of another magnet, they attract. If you put two north poles together, then the magnets will repel each other. The same thing happens when you put two south poles together.

Scientists have a rule to help you remember: Like poles repel, unlike poles attract.

Temporary Magnets

Temporary magnets do not have a magnetic field around them all the time. An electromagnet is a temporary magnet. Most electromagnets are made when electricity flows through a coil of wire that has been wrapped around an iron or steel core. It only attracts metals while the electric current flows. When the current stops, so does the magnetism.

Electromagnets are often used in switches on doorbells and telegraphs. They can also run refrigerators, washing machines, CD players, and toys like electric trains, robots, and race cars. Large electromagnets can be attached to cranes. When the electricity is on, they are strong enough to pick up cars and move them from place to place.

As you can see, magnetism is a powerful invisible force!

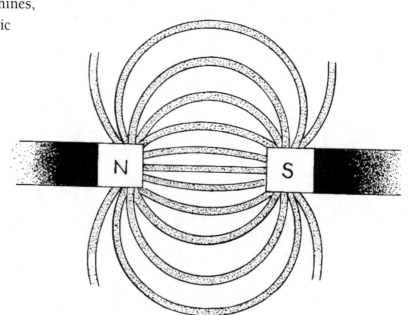

Name _____

An Invisible Force

Fill in the bubble to answer each question or complete each sentence.

1. Magnetism is an invisible force that can make certain objects _____.
   Ⓐ move toward each other
   Ⓑ move away from each other
   Ⓒ move toward each other or move away from each other
   Ⓓ not move at all

2. Which of these four metals is <u>not</u> found in magnets?
   Ⓐ iron
   Ⓑ nickel
   Ⓒ lead
   Ⓓ steel

3. What is the rule about the strength of magnetism?
   Ⓐ The north pole and south pole make an electric current.
   Ⓑ All magnets have the same magnetic power.
   Ⓒ Like poles attract, unlike poles repel.
   Ⓓ Like poles repel, unlike poles attract.

4. A permanent magnet is surrounded by a magnetic field _____.
   Ⓐ all of the time
   Ⓑ most of the time
   Ⓒ some of the time
   Ⓓ only when electricity flows through it

5. Electromagnets can work only when the magnet has _____.
   Ⓐ an electric current that has been turned off
   Ⓑ an electric current flowing through it
   Ⓒ a north and south pole
   Ⓓ another permanent magnet attached to it

Bonus: On the back of this page, write a paragraph about electromagnets and how they work.

The Study of Magnetism

Magnets are objects that have an invisible force called magnetism. Magnetism draws certain metals (iron, nickel, cobalt, and steel) to magnets. The area around a magnet where the force can be felt is called the magnetic field.

Early Discoveries

Magnetism was first discovered in an iron ore called magnetite. People in ancient Greece and China found that magnetite pieces attracted other metals to it. The Chinese also discovered that magnetite would point in a north-south direction. This led to the invention of the first compass.

In 1600, William Gilbert concluded that Earth itself was a giant magnet with north and south poles. Then in 1820, Hans Christian Oersted observed that an electric current flowing through a wire caused the needle of a magnetic compass to rotate. His discovery proved there was a connection between electricity and magnetism.

More Discoveries

From that time on, the study of magnets has led to more discoveries and inventions. Scientists have discovered that pigeons, bees, salmon, dolphins, and tuna use magnetite in their bodies. The magnetite helps them know where to migrate!

Simple permanent magnets are in such everyday objects as latches for doors and paper fasteners. Permanent magnets are ones that always have a magnetic field around them.

Electromagnets are called temporary magnets. Most electromagnets are made when electricity goes through a coil of wire that has been wrapped around an iron core. It only attracts metals while the electric current is flowing. There are electromagnets in household objects such as electric doorbells and refrigerators.

Magnets in Industry, Business, and Medicine

Electromagnets are in such things as computers, photocopiers, and machine tools. Generators in power plants rely on these magnets. Electromagnets help move trains and subways. Cranes use giant electromagnets to move steel beams and cars. Doctors use electromagnets. A procedure called Magnetic Resonance Imaging (MRI) produces images of the body. This helps to see the cause of the problem inside the person.

Scientists continue to work to make magnets more and more powerful.

Nonfiction Reading Practice, Grade 5 • EMC 3316 • ©2003 by Evan-Moor Corp.

Name _____

The Study of Magnetism

Fill in the bubble to answer each question or complete each sentence.

1. Magnetism draws certain metals to metals. Those metals are _____.
   - Ⓐ only iron and steel
   - Ⓑ gold, silver, lead, and zinc
   - Ⓒ iron, nickel, cobalt, and steel
   - Ⓓ iron, nickel, cobalt, and silver

2. What led to the discovery of magnetism?
   - Ⓐ Ancient people found a natural magnet called magnetite.
   - Ⓑ William Gilbert found that Earth was magnetic.
   - Ⓒ Hans Christian Oersted discovered electric magnets.
   - Ⓓ People found magnets in compasses.

3. Some animals use magnetite in their bodies to know where to _____.
   - Ⓐ find food
   - Ⓑ hide from predators
   - Ⓒ find a mate
   - Ⓓ migrate

4. Which group of words describes electromagnets?
   - Ⓐ magnetite, lodestone, compass
   - Ⓑ electric current, wire, iron core
   - Ⓒ trains, subways, escalators
   - Ⓓ industry, business, medicine

5. Magnetic Resonance Imaging (MRI) is used for producing _____.
   - Ⓐ strong magnets
   - Ⓑ compasses
   - Ⓒ images of a person
   - Ⓓ generators

Bonus: Imagine you have just been asked to come up with a new invention using a magnet. On the back of this page, describe your new invention and how it works. Include a picture of your new invention, too.

Brine Shrimp

Introducing the Topic

1. Reproduce page 55 for individual students, or make a transparency to use with a group or the whole class.

2. Show students the pictures of the female and male brine shrimp. Share with students that the word brine means "salty." Discuss the fact that most shrimp live in the salty ocean. But brine shrimp also live in salty lakes, and some even live in desert areas. Then discuss the diagram of the female brine shrimp and the unusual way they eat.

Reading the Selections

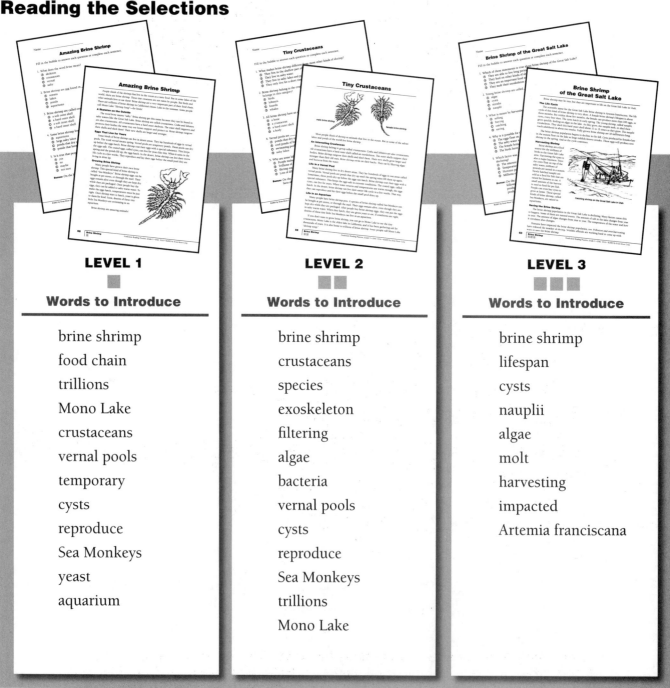

LEVEL 1

Words to Introduce

brine shrimp

food chain

trillions

Mono Lake

crustaceans

vernal pools

temporary

cysts

reproduce

Sea Monkeys

yeast

aquarium

LEVEL 2

Words to Introduce

brine shrimp

crustaceans

species

exoskeleton

filtering

algae

bacteria

vernal pools

cysts

reproduce

Sea Monkeys

trillions

Mono Lake

LEVEL 3

Words to Introduce

brine shrimp

lifespan

cysts

nauplii

algae

molt

harvesting

impacted

Artemia franciscana

Brine Shrimp

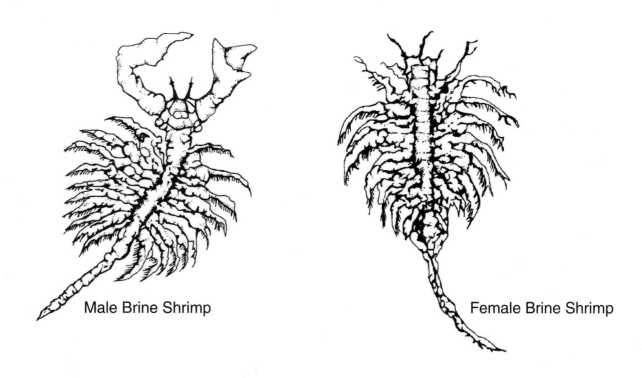

Male Brine Shrimp

Female Brine Shrimp

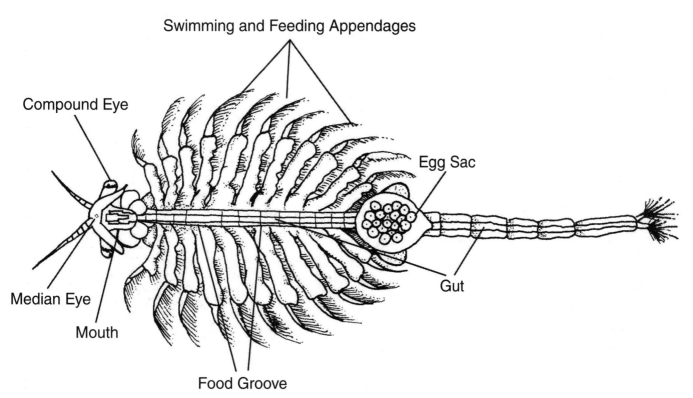

Swimming and Feeding Appendages

Compound Eye

Egg Sac

Median Eye

Gut

Mouth

Food Groove

Brine shrimp have an unusual way of eating their food. They move their appendages back and forth. This causes a current in the water. Water filled with algae flows through the posterior end of the food groove. The algae moves through the food groove to the mouth.

Amazing Brine Shrimp

People think of the shrimp that live in the ocean as a tasty food. But in some lakes of the world, there are brine shrimp. These tiny creatures are not eaten by people. But birds and other animals love to eat them! Brine shrimp are a very important part of their food chain. There are trillions of brine shrimp in California's Mono Lake in the summer. Some people call Mono Lake "shrimp soup"—for birds!

A Skeleton on the Outside

The word brine means "salty." Brine shrimp get this name because they can be found in salty waters like the Great Salt Lake. Brine shrimp are called crustaceans. Crabs and lobsters are also crustaceans. All crustaceans have a hard outer skeleton. The outer shell supports and protects their bodies the same way our bones support and protect us. Brine shrimp outgrow their shells and shed them! Their new shells are larger and stronger.

Eggs That Live for Years

Some kinds of brine shrimp can live in desert areas. They lay hundreds of eggs in vernal pools. The word *vernal* means "spring." Vernal pools are temporary ponds. These pools can dry up before the eggs hatch. Brine shrimp coat their eggs with a special substance. This keeps the eggs safe. The coated eggs, called cysts, can live for years like this. When it rains in the spring and the ponds fill up, the eggs hatch. In the desert, brine shrimp can live their entire life cycle in a few weeks. They reproduce and lay their eggs before the small pool they are living in dries up.

Growing Brine Shrimp

Many people have grown their own brine shrimp. This special kind of brine shrimp is called "Sea Monkeys." Brine shrimp eggs can be bought at pet stores, or through the mail. Their eggs remain alive even though they are kept dry while they are packaged. Once people buy the eggs, they can be added to warm salty water. To make the eggs hatch, temperatures must be just right. Once shrimp start to hatch, yeast is given to them for food. Soon, dozens of these tiny little Sea Monkeys are swimming in an aquarium.

Brine shrimp are amazing animals!

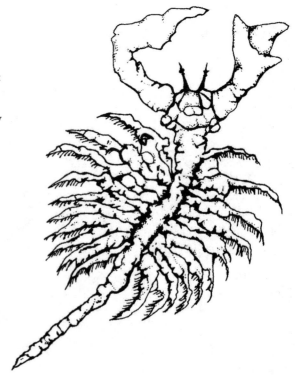

Nonfiction Reading Practice, Grade 5 • EMC 3316 • ©2003 by Evan-Moor Corp.

Amazing Brine Shrimp

Fill in the bubble to answer each question or complete each sentence.

1. What does the word brine mean?
   - Ⓐ skeleton
   - Ⓑ crustacean
   - Ⓒ vernal
   - Ⓓ salty

2. Brine shrimp are <u>not</u> found in _____.
   - Ⓐ oceans
   - Ⓑ lakes
   - Ⓒ ponds
   - Ⓓ aquariums

3. Brine shrimp are called crustaceans because they have _____.
   - Ⓐ a soft outer shell
   - Ⓑ a hard outer shell
   - Ⓒ a soft inner shell
   - Ⓓ a hard inner shell

4. Some brine shrimp live in vernal pools. Vernal pools are _____.
   - Ⓐ aquariums
   - Ⓑ large salty lakes
   - Ⓒ ponds that dry up and then fill up in the spring
   - Ⓓ ponds that have lots of water in them all the time

5. Is it true that people can really grow Sea Monkeys?
   - Ⓐ yes
   - Ⓑ no
   - Ⓒ maybe
   - Ⓓ not sure

Bonus: On the back of this page, write the steps to follow to grow Sea Monkeys.

Tiny Crustaceans

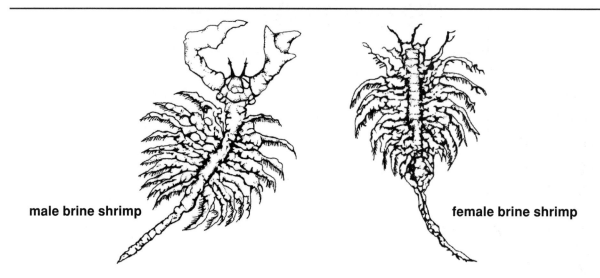

male brine shrimp

female brine shrimp

Most people think of shrimp as animals that live in the ocean. But in some of the warmer, saltier lakes and ponds of the world live brine shrimp.

An Interesting Crustacean

Brine shrimp belong to a group called crustaceans. Crabs and lobsters are also crustaceans. All crustaceans have a hard outer shell called an exoskeleton. The outer shells support their bodies. Brine shrimp outgrow their shells and shed them. Their new shells grow larger and stronger than their old ones. Brine shrimp swim on their backs. They eat by filtering algae and bacteria from the water.

Life in a Vernal Pool

Many brine shrimp live in dry desert areas. They lay hundreds of eggs in wet areas called vernal pools. Vernal pools are ponds that dry up until the spring rains fill them up again. Sometimes, these pools dry up before the eggs can hatch. Brine shrimp coat their eggs with a special substance. This keeps the eggs safe in extreme conditions. The coated eggs, called cysts, can live for years. When water returns and temperatures are warm enough, the eggs hatch. In the desert, brine shrimp can live their entire life cycle in a few weeks. That way, they can reproduce and lay their eggs before the small pool dries up.

Life in an Aquarium

Many people have brine shrimp pets. A species of brine shrimp called Sea Monkeys can be bought at pet stores, or through the mail. Their eggs remain alive, even though they are kept dry while they are packaged. After people buy brine shrimp eggs, they can put the eggs in warm salty water. When they hatch, they are given yeast to eat. If conditions are right, dozens of these tiny little Sea Monkeys can live in an aquarium.

If you don't want to grow brine shrimp, you can go to Mono Lake to see the tiny crustaceans. Mono Lake is the oldest lake in California, and it has been gathering salt for thousands of years. It is also home to trillions of brine shrimp. Some people call Mono Lake "shrimp soup."

Nonfiction Reading Practice, Grade 5 • EMC 3316 • ©2003 by Evan-Moor Corp.

Name _____

Tiny Crustaceans

Fill in the bubble to answer each question or complete each sentence.

1. What makes brine shrimp different from most other kinds of shrimp?
   - Ⓐ They live in the shallow part of oceans.
   - Ⓑ They live in the deep part of oceans.
   - Ⓒ They live in salty lakes and ponds.
   - Ⓓ They only live for a short time.

2. Brine shrimp belong to the crustacean family. Which of these animals also belongs in this category?
   - Ⓐ birds
   - Ⓑ lobsters
   - Ⓒ lizards
   - Ⓓ whales

3. All brine shrimp have an exoskeleton. What is an exoskeleton?
   - Ⓐ a bone
   - Ⓑ a crustacean
   - Ⓒ a hard outer shell
   - Ⓓ a body

4. Vernal pools are _____.
   - Ⓐ ponds that dry up until spring rains fill them up
   - Ⓑ cool ponds of fresh water
   - Ⓒ swimming pools
   - Ⓓ salty lakes

5. Why are some lakes like Mono Lake called "shrimp soup"?
   - Ⓐ People make soup out of the water.
   - Ⓑ Trillions of brine shrimp live in the water.
   - Ⓒ Brine shrimp eat other shrimp there.
   - Ⓓ Lots of different kinds of shrimp live there.

Bonus: On the back of this page, draw a picture of a brine shrimp. Write five facts about it under the picture.

Brine Shrimp of the Great Salt Lake

Brine shrimp may be tiny, but they are important to life on the Great Salt Lake in Utah.

The Life Cycle

The scientific name for the Great Salt Lake brine shrimp is Artemia franciscana. The life cycle of this kind of brine shrimp is very short. A female brine shrimp's lifespan is about three months. But within those few months, the female can produce more than 100 eggs, or cysts, every four days. The cysts hatch in early spring. The young shrimp, called nauplii, grow quickly, feeding on algae in the lake. As they grow, the nauplii molt, or shed their exoskeleton. They shed this hard outer shell about 11 to 15 times as they grow. The nauplii reach adulthood in about two weeks. Fully grown brine shrimp are 10 millimeters long.

The brine shrimp population begins to decline in the fall. Cysts produced by females late in the season float on the lake as large reddish-brown streaks. These eggs will produce new shrimp in the spring. And so the cycle continues.

Harvesting Shrimp

Brine shrimp are a food source for the millions of birds in the Great Salt Lake area. Harvesting the cysts is also a major business. Since the cysts float on top of the salty water, millions of pounds are netted in a season. Newly hatched nauplii are sold as food for fish that are raised for humans to eat. A small amount of the harvest is used as food for pet fish. People can even buy cysts to grow at home. These special kinds of brine shrimp, called Sea Monkeys, are raised in aquariums.

Harvesting shrimp eggs on the Great Salt Lake in Utah

Saving the Brine Shrimp

The brine shrimp population in the Great Salt Lake is declining. Many factors cause this to happen. Some of them are natural events. The amount of salt in the lake changes from year to year. The amount of algae changes from year to year. The temperature of the water and how it circulates also changes.

Humans have impacted the brine shrimp population, too. Pollution and over-harvesting have reduced the number of shrimp. Wildlife officials are working hard to come up with ways to save the brine shrimp.

Nonfiction Reading Practice, Grade 5 • EMC 3316 • ©2003 by Evan-Moor Corp.

Brine Shrimp of the Great Salt Lake

Fill in the bubble to answer each question or complete each sentence.

1. Which of these statements is true about brine shrimp of the Great Salt Lake?
   - Ⓐ They are able to live long periods of time.
   - Ⓑ They feed on other kinds of shrimp in the lake.
   - Ⓒ They are an important food source for birds.
   - Ⓓ They molt their exoskeleton once in a lifetime.

2. Young brine shrimp are called _____.
   - Ⓐ algae
   - Ⓑ cysts
   - Ⓒ streaks
   - Ⓓ nauplii

3. What is meant by *harvesting* brine shrimp cysts?
   - Ⓐ selling
   - Ⓑ buying
   - Ⓒ catching
   - Ⓓ saving

4. Why is it possible for the fishermen to easily catch the cysts?
   - Ⓐ The eggs float on top of the salty water.
   - Ⓑ The salty water and the cysts are the same color.
   - Ⓒ The female brine shrimp lay the eggs near the shore.
   - Ⓓ The birds leave the exoskeletons of the eggs behind.

5. Which factor was <u>not</u> given to explain why brine shrimp populations are declining?
   - Ⓐ The amount of salt in the lake may be different from year to year.
   - Ⓑ Temperatures in the lake change from year to year.
   - Ⓒ Humans pollute the Great Salt Lake area.
   - Ⓓ Millions of birds eat too many of the brine shrimp.

Bonus: On the back of this page, solve the following math problem. Show the steps you followed to find the answer. The female brine shrimp lives 90 days. She produces 100 cysts every 4 days. What is the total number of cysts she produces in her lifetime?

The Water Cycle

Introducing the Topic

1. Reproduce page 63 for individual students, or make a transparency to use with a group or the whole class.

2. Discuss the idea that the amount of water on Earth doesn't change. New water is not created; in fact, the water that falls as rain today may be the same water that dinosaurs used millions of years ago. Water is constantly being recycled through a process called the water cycle. Show students the diagram of the water cycle and tell them to refer back to this diagram as they read the articles.

Reading the Selections

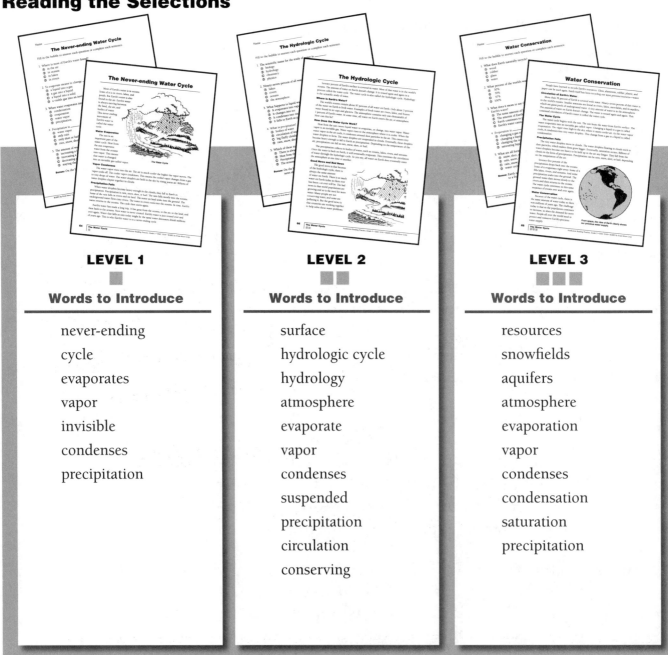

LEVEL 1

Words to Introduce

never-ending

cycle

evaporates

vapor

invisible

condenses

precipitation

LEVEL 2

Words to Introduce

surface

hydrologic cycle

hydrology

atmosphere

evaporate

vapor

condenses

suspended

precipitation

circulation

conserving

LEVEL 3

Words to Introduce

resources

snowfields

aquifers

atmosphere

evaporation

vapor

condenses

condensation

saturation

precipitation

The Water Cycle

1. Heat from the sun evaporates liquid water from Earth's surface.

2. Liquid water evaporates into an invisible gas called water vapor.

3. Water vapor rises above Earth where the air is cooler.

4. Water vapor cools and condenses around dust particles. Tiny water droplets are formed in clouds.

5. Eventually these droplets become heavy enough to fall from the clouds to Earth as precipitation. Depending on the temperature, precipitation can fall as rain, snow, sleet, or hail.

Once the precipitation is back on Earth, it will eventually evaporate, thus continuing the water cycle. The amount of water on Earth doesn't change. The water is just reused again and again.

The Never-ending Water Cycle

Most of Earth's water is in oceans. Some of it is in rivers, lakes, and ponds. But Earth's water is also found in the air. Earth's water is always moving between the land, the air, and the bodies of water. This never-ending movement of Earth's water is called the water cycle.

Water Evaporates

The sun is an important part of the water cycle. Heat from the sun evaporates water from the oceans into vapor. This means that water is changed into an invisible gas called vapor.

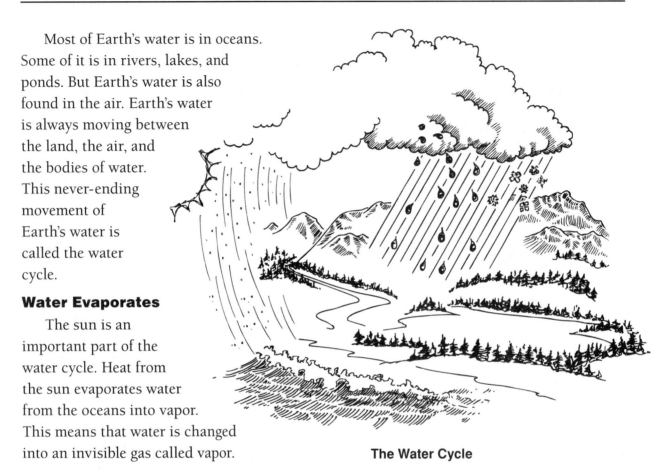

The Water Cycle

Vapor Condenses

The water vapor rises into the air. The air is much cooler the higher the vapor moves. The vapor cools off. The cooler vapor condenses. This means the cooled vapor changes from a gas to tiny drops of water. The water droplets are held in the sky by rising warm air. Billions of water droplets cluster together in clouds.

Precipitation Falls

When water droplets become heavy enough in the clouds, they fall to Earth as precipitation. Precipitation is rain, snow, sleet, or hail. The rain falls mostly into the oceans. Some of the rain falls into rivers and onto land. The water on land sinks into the ground. The underground water flows into rivers. The water in rivers runs into the oceans. In time, Earth's water returns to the oceans. The cycle then starts again.

Earth's water has made a long trip. It has gone from the oceans, to the air, to the land, and then back to the oceans. New water is never created. Earth's water is just reused over and over again. Water that falls as rain today might be the same water dinosaurs drank millions of years ago. This is why Earth's water is in a never-ending cycle.

Nonfiction Reading Practice, Grade 5 • EMC 3316 • ©2003 by Evan-Moor Corp.

Name _____

The Never-ending Water Cycle

Fill in the bubble to answer each question or complete each sentence.

1. Where is most of Earth's water found?
   - Ⓐ in the air
   - Ⓑ in oceans
   - Ⓒ in lakes
   - Ⓓ in rivers

2. To evaporate means to change _____.
   - Ⓐ a liquid into a gas
   - Ⓑ a gas into a liquid
   - Ⓒ a liquid into a solid
   - Ⓓ a visible gas into an invisible gas

3. When water evaporates into an invisible gas, it is called _____.
   - Ⓐ condensation
   - Ⓑ evaporation
   - Ⓒ water vapor
   - Ⓓ precipitation

4. Precipitation is _____.
   - Ⓐ water vapor
   - Ⓑ only rain
   - Ⓒ only sleet or hail
   - Ⓓ rain, snow, sleet, or hail

5. The amount of water found on Earth is _____.
   - Ⓐ increasing a little
   - Ⓑ increasing a lot
   - Ⓒ decreasing a lot
   - Ⓓ staying the same

Bonus: On the back of this page, draw and label a picture of the water cycle.

The Hydrologic Cycle

Seventy percent of Earth's surface is covered in water. Most of that water is in the world's oceans. The amount of water on Earth doesn't change. It is reused again and again in a process called the water cycle. The water cycle is also called the hydrologic cycle. Hydrology is the scientific study of water.

Where Is Earth's Water?

The world's oceans contain about 97 percent of all water on Earth. Only about 3 percent of the water on Earth is fresh water. Examples of fresh water are rivers, lakes, and frozen water found in ice caps and glaciers. The atmosphere contains only one-thousandth of 1 percent of Earth's water. At some time, all water on Earth enters the air, or atmosphere. How can this be?

How Does the Water Cycle Work?

Heat from the sun causes liquid water to evaporate, or change, into water vapor. Water vapor is an invisible gas. Water vapor rises to the atmosphere where it is cooler. When the water vapor in the air cools, it condenses around dust particles in the air. This causes tiny water droplets to form. The water droplets are suspended in clouds. Eventually, these droplets become heavy enough to fall to Earth as precipitation. Depending on the temperature of the air, precipitation can fall as rain, snow, sleet, or hail.

The precipitation collects in bodies of water, such as oceans, lakes, rivers, and streams. Once the water is back on Earth, it will eventually evaporate. This continues the circulation of water through the hydrologic cycle. So you see, all water on Earth does eventually enter the atmosphere at one time or another.

Good News and Bad News

The good news is that because of the hydrologic cycle, there is always the same amount of water on Earth. There is as much water on Earth today as there ever has been—or ever will be. The bad news is that world populations are growing and so is the need for more water. Many people are not conserving water, and some are polluting it. But the good news is that countries are working together to help solve these water problems.

Name _____

The Hydrologic Cycle

Fill in the bubble to answer each question or complete each sentence.

1. The scientific name for the study of water is _____.
   - Ⓐ biology
   - Ⓑ hydrology
   - Ⓒ chemistry
   - Ⓓ physics

2. Ninety-seven percent of all water on Earth is located in _____.
   - Ⓐ lakes
   - Ⓑ rivers
   - Ⓒ the oceans
   - Ⓓ the atmosphere

3. What happens to liquid water when it is heated by the sun?
   - Ⓐ It evaporates into vapor.
   - Ⓑ It changes into ice.
   - Ⓒ It condenses into tiny water droplets.
   - Ⓓ It falls to Earth as precipitation.

4. What is precipitation?
   - Ⓐ bodies of water
   - Ⓑ circulation of water
   - Ⓒ big fluffy clouds
   - Ⓓ rain, snow, sleet, or hail

5. Which of these statements is true about the hydrologic cycle?
   - Ⓐ There is always the same amount of water on Earth.
   - Ⓑ Heat from the sun causes water vapor to change into liquid water.
   - Ⓒ Precipitation only falls on oceans.
   - Ⓓ The atmosphere contains most of Earth's water.

Bonus: On the back of this page, write a paragraph telling the good and bad news about Earth's water supply.

Water Conservation

People have learned to recycle Earth's resources. Glass, aluminum, rubber, plastic, and paper can be used again. Earth itself has been recycling our most precious resource—water.

Circulation of Earth's Water

More than 70 percent of Earth is covered with water. Ninety-seven percent of this water is in the world's oceans. Smaller amounts are found in rivers, lakes, snowfields, and in aquifers, which are giant pools of underground water. A tiny amount of water is in the atmosphere. The amount of water on Earth doesn't change. The water is reused again and again. This continuous circulation of Earth's water is called the water cycle.

The Water Cycle

The water cycle begins with the sun. The sun heats the water on Earth's surface. The water evaporates into an invisible gas called vapor. Changing a liquid to a gas is called evaporation. The vapor rises high in the sky, where it meets cooler air. As the water vapor cools, it condenses into tiny water droplets. This change from a gas to a liquid is called condensation.

Precipitation Falls

The tiny water droplets form in the clouds. The water droplets in the clouds stick to dust particles, which makes them grow bigger. Eventually, saturation occurs. Billions of water droplets become too heavy to be held up in the air any longer. They fall from the clouds in the form of precipitation. Precipitation can be rain, snow, sleet, or hail, depending on the temperature of the air.

Seventy-five percent of the precipitation drops back into the oceans. Some of it evaporates right away. Some of it fills lakes, rivers, and streams. And some precipitation soaks into the ground. The ground water then moves slowly to the rivers and then returns to the oceans. The water cycle continues in this same sequence of events over and over again.

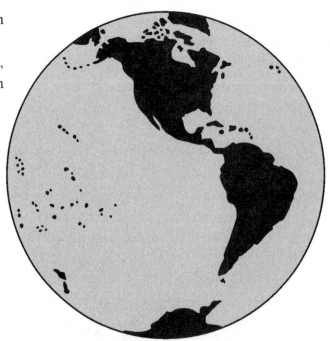

From space, the view of Earth clearly shows our precious water supply.

Water Conservation

Because of the water cycle, there is the same amount of water today as there was millions of years ago. The challenge today is that as the population continues to increase, so does the demand for more water. People all over the world need to protect and conserve Earth's precious water supply.

Name _____

Water Conservation

Fill in the bubble to answer each question or complete each sentence.

1. What does Earth naturally recycle?
   - Ⓐ wood
   - Ⓑ rubber
   - Ⓒ glass
   - Ⓓ water

2. What percent of the world's water is in the oceans?
   - Ⓐ 50%
   - Ⓑ 70%
   - Ⓒ 97%
   - Ⓓ 100%

3. What does it mean to say that the water cycle is a continuous circulation of Earth's water?
   - Ⓐ The same amount of Earth's water is reused again and again.
   - Ⓑ The amount of Earth's water changes all the time.
   - Ⓒ Earth continues to produce more and more water.
   - Ⓓ Earth's water cannot be recycled.

4. Evaporation is _____ and condensation is _____.
   - Ⓐ changing a gas to a liquid; changing a liquid to a gas
   - Ⓑ changing a liquid to a gas; changing a gas to a liquid
   - Ⓒ changing the temperature of the air; keeping the temperature constant
   - Ⓓ saturating liquids; making precipitation fall

5. What are all forms of precipitation?
   - Ⓐ snow, sleet, and hail
   - Ⓑ rain, snow, sleet, and temperature
   - Ⓒ rain, snow, sleet, and hail
   - Ⓓ water cycle

Bonus: Earth naturally recycles water. On the back of this page, write a letter to a friend explaining ways you conserve Earth's water.

Cloud Seeding

Introducing the Topic

1. Reproduce page 71 for individual students, or make a transparency to use with a group or the whole class.

2. Discuss with students the increased need for more water on Earth. This is due to growing populations around the world that have to share water supplies. Tell students that scientists have discovered a method that actually increases precious water supplies. Show the cloud seeding sequence diagram. Discuss how the cloud-seeding process works. Tell students they will learn more about this artificial way of making water fall from a cloud.

Reading the Selections

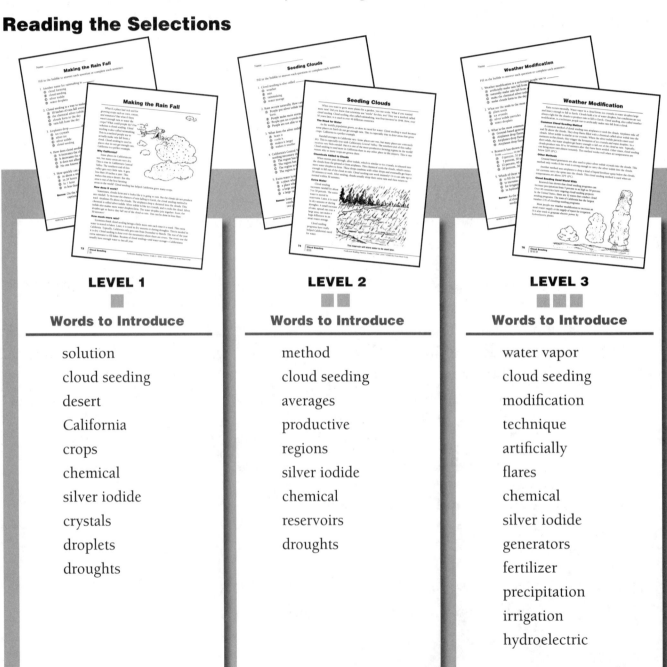

LEVEL 1
■

Words to Introduce

solution

cloud seeding

desert

California

crops

chemical

silver iodide

crystals

droplets

droughts

LEVEL 2
■ ■

Words to Introduce

method

cloud seeding

averages

productive

regions

silver iodide

chemical

reservoirs

droughts

LEVEL 3
■ ■ ■

Words to Introduce

water vapor

cloud seeding

modification

technique

artificially

flares

chemical

silver iodide

generators

fertilizer

precipitation

irrigation

hydroelectric

Cloud Seeding

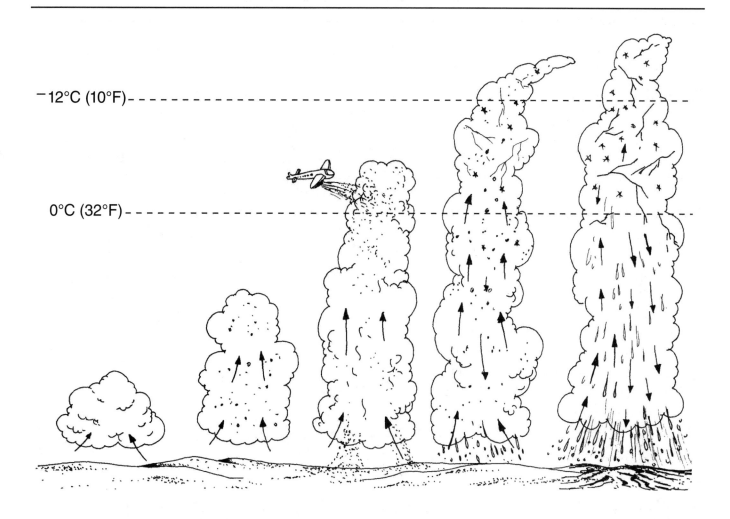

−12°C (10°F)

0°C (32°F)

5 minutes	10 minutes	15 minutes	20 minutes	30 minutes
A cumulus cloud begins to develop.	A few large water droplets form. The cloud grows.	An airplane drops flares filled with silver iodide particles into the cloud. This seeding agent cools the cloud and helps more water droplets to form.	The cloud is heavy with more water droplets and ice particles. It has begun to rain.	Seeding the cloud has helped to make it release more rain to Earth.

©2003 by Evan-Moor Corp. • Nonfiction Reading Practice, Grade 5 • EMC 3316

Making the Rain Fall

What if a place had rich soil for growing crops such as corn, cotton, and tomatoes? But what if there wasn't enough rain to water the crops? What could people do? One solution is cloud seeding. Cloud seeding is also called rainmaking. This is a method people use to actually make rain fall from a cloud. Cloud seeding is used in places that do not get enough rain. California is a perfect example.

Why California?

Some places in California are wet, but many areas are very dry. This is true in California's Central Valley. The southern end of this valley gets very little rain. It gets less than 10 inches a year. This makes this area a desert. But this area is one of the best farming areas in the world! Cloud seeding has helped California grow many crops.

How does it work?

Sometimes, clouds form and it looks like it is going to rain. But the clouds do not produce any rainfall. To increase the chances of rain falling to Earth, the cloud-seeding method is used. Airplanes fly above the clouds. The airplanes drop a chemical into the clouds. This chemical is called silver iodide. Silver iodide is like ice crystals, and it cools the cloud. Silver iodide also makes more water droplets form. The water droplets join together. Soon, the droplets get so heavy they fall out of the cloud as rain. This can all happen in less than 30 minutes!

How much more rain?

Scientists think cloud seeding brings a little more rain each time it is used. This extra water is stored in lakes. Later, it is used in dry seasons or during droughts. This is needed in California. Typically, California only gets rain from December to March. The rest of the year it is dry. Cloud seeding is done over the mountains where there are rivers. The rivers use the extra rainwater to fill lakes. Because of cloud seeding—and water storage—Californians usually have enough water to last all year.

Name _____

Making the Rain Fall

Fill in the bubble to answer each question or complete each sentence.

1. Another name for rainmaking is _____.
   - Ⓐ cloud forming
   - Ⓑ cloud seeding
   - Ⓒ silver iodide
   - Ⓓ water droplets

2. Cloud seeding is a way to make _____.
   - Ⓐ 10 inches of rain fall every time
   - Ⓑ the chemical silver iodide
   - Ⓒ clouds form in the sky
   - Ⓓ rain fall from the sky

3. Airplanes drop _____ above the clouds to help form water droplets.
   - Ⓐ ice crystals
   - Ⓑ silver ice
   - Ⓒ silver iodide
   - Ⓓ seeds

4. How does cloud seeding affect the chances of rain falling on Earth?
   - Ⓐ It increases the chance of rain.
   - Ⓑ It decreases the chance of rain.
   - Ⓒ It does not affect the chance of rain in any way.
   - Ⓓ No one knows for sure.

5. How quickly can a seeded cloud produce more rain?
   - Ⓐ in about a week
   - Ⓑ in 24 hours
   - Ⓒ in 1 hour
   - Ⓓ in less than 30 minutes

Bonus: On the back of this page, draw a picture of cloud seeding. Write a caption under the picture explaining how cloud seeding works.

Seeding Clouds

When you want to grow more plants for a garden, you use seeds. What if you wanted more rain? Did you know that scientists use "seeds" for this, too? They use a method called cloud seeding. Cloud seeding, also called rainmaking, was first invented in 1946. Now, over 50 years later, it is used in over 40 different countries.

The Need for Water

As the world's population grows, so does its need for water. Cloud seeding is used because some places on Earth do not get enough rain. This is especially true in drier areas that grow crops. California is a perfect example.

Rainfall averages in California vary. Some places are wet, but many places are extremely dry. This is especially true with California's Central Valley. The southern end of this valley receives very little rainfall. But it is one of the most productive farming regions in the world! Cloud seeding is used more in California than in any other place in the country. This is one reason why so many crops are grown there.

Chemicals Added to Clouds

When storms pass through, silver iodide, which is similar to ice crystals, is released into the clouds from the ground or from airplanes. This chemical cools the clouds, which causes more water droplets to form. These drops combine with other drops and eventually get heavy enough to fall out of the cloud as rain. Cloud seeding can work instantly! Or it can take up to 30 minutes to work. After seeding, clouds usually drop their extra rain and then return to normal within 30 minutes.

Extra Water

Cloud seeding increases rainfall by about 5 to 30 percent. The extra water is stored in reservoirs. Later, it is used in dry seasons or during droughts. A small increase of rain, spread out over a large area, can make a huge difference in an area's water storage.

Cloud-seeding programs have really helped California's need for water.

The reservoir will store water to be used later.

Nonfiction Reading Practice, Grade 5 • EMC 3316 • ©2003 by Evan-Moor Corp.

Name _____

Seeding Clouds

Fill in the bubble to answer each question or complete each sentence.

1. Cloud seeding is also called _____.
   - Ⓐ weather
   - Ⓑ rain
   - Ⓒ rainmaking
   - Ⓓ water storage

2. Rain occurs naturally. How can people make it rain?
   - Ⓐ People put silver iodide into clouds, which causes more water droplets to form.
   - Ⓑ People make more storm clouds form in the sky.
   - Ⓒ People put extra water droplets into clouds.
   - Ⓓ People are not able to make rain.

3. What does the silver iodide do to a cloud?
   - Ⓐ heats it
   - Ⓑ cools it
   - Ⓒ makes it larger
   - Ⓓ makes it smaller

4. California's Central Valley is a very productive farming region. Why is cloud seeding necessary there?
   - Ⓐ The region has lots of farm animals.
   - Ⓑ The region has farms.
   - Ⓒ The region is very wet.
   - Ⓓ The region is extremely dry.

5. Extra water is stored in reservoirs. What is a *reservoir*?
   - Ⓐ a place where large quantities of water are stored
   - Ⓑ a place where scientists study water use
   - Ⓒ a large storm cloud
   - Ⓓ a large valley

Bonus: Some people don't like the idea of cloud seeding. They think increased rainfall might cause too many problems. On the back of this page, write two problems that increased rainfall might cause.

Weather Modification

Rain occurs naturally. Water vapor in a cloud forms ice crystals or water droplets large and heavy enough to fall to Earth. Clouds hold a lot of water droplets, but conditions are not always right for the clouds to produce rain to fall to Earth. Cloud seeding, also called weather modification, is a technique people use to artificially make rain fall from a cloud.

Common Cloud-Seeding Method

A common method of cloud seeding uses airplanes to seed the clouds. Airplanes take off and fly above the clouds. They drop flares filled with a chemical called silver iodide into the clouds. Silver iodide is similar to ice crystals. When the silver iodide particles meet cool moisture in the clouds, they trigger the formation of ice crystals and water droplets. In a short while, the water droplets get heavy enough to fall out of the clouds as rain. Typically, clouds produce rain 20 to 30 minutes after they have been seeded. Other times, cloud seeding can bring more rain almost instantly. This method works well when air temperatures are below 32°F (0°C).

Other Methods

Ground-based generators are also used to place silver iodide crystals in the clouds. This method only works if the wind is strong enough to carry the silver iodide up into the clouds.

Another method uses airplanes to drop a kind of liquid fertilizer spray below the clouds. Air currents carry the spray into the clouds. This cloud-seeding method is used when air temperatures are above 32°F (0°C).

Cloud Seeding Used World Wide

Research has shown that cloud-seeding programs can increase precipitation from 5 percent to as high as 30 percent. Over 40 countries have ongoing cloud-seeding projects. In the United States, there are 12 states that conduct cloud-seeding programs. The state of California has the largest number (15) of cloud-seeding programs.

Most people use weather modification to increase an area's water supply or its supply of water for irrigation. It is also used to generate electric power by hydroelectric plants.

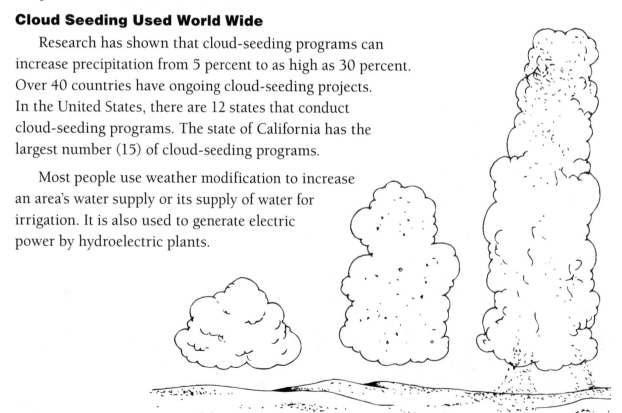

Name _____

Weather Modification

Fill in the bubble to answer each question or complete each sentence.

1. Weather modification is a technique people use to _____.
   Ⓐ artificially make rain fall from a cloud
   Ⓑ naturally make rain fall from a cloud
   Ⓒ make the chemical silver iodide
   Ⓓ make clouds form in the sky

2. What are the seeds in the most common cloud-seeding method?
   Ⓐ plant seeds
   Ⓑ air currents
   Ⓒ silver iodide particles
   Ⓓ water droplets

3. What is the most common method of rainmaking?
   Ⓐ Ground-based generators place silver iodide crystals in the clouds.
   Ⓑ Airplanes drop flares of liquid fertilizer from below the clouds.
   Ⓒ Airplanes drop flares of silver iodide particles from below the clouds.
   Ⓓ Airplanes drop flares of silver iodide particles from above the clouds.

4. Research has shown that cloud-seeding programs can increase precipitation
   from _____ to as high as _____.
   Ⓐ 0 percent, 32 percent
   Ⓑ 5 percent, 30 percent
   Ⓒ 12 percent, 40 percent
   Ⓓ 20 percent, 30 percent

5. Which of these uses for water is not mentioned in the article?
   Ⓐ to fill the oceans
   Ⓑ to increase an area's water supply
   Ⓒ for irrigation
   Ⓓ in hydroelectric plants

Bonus: As the world's population grows, so does the need for water. On the back
of this page, write a newspaper story telling why the use of cloud seeding
is important to the world.

John Muir

Introducing the Topic

1. Reproduce page 79 for individual students, or make a transparency to use with a group or the whole class.

2. Show students the time line of John Muir's life. Tell students John Muir was one of America's most famous and influential naturalists and conservationists. Share with students that John Muir is called the "Father of our National Parks."

Reading the Selections

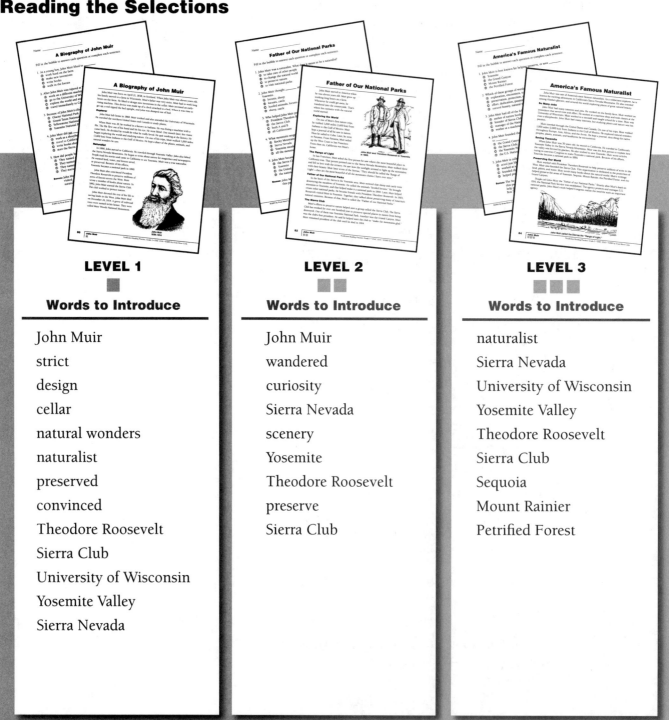

LEVEL 1

Words to Introduce

John Muir

strict

design

cellar

natural wonders

naturalist

preserved

convinced

Theodore Roosevelt

Sierra Club

University of Wisconsin

Yosemite Valley

Sierra Nevada

LEVEL 2

Words to Introduce

John Muir

wandered

curiosity

Sierra Nevada

scenery

Yosemite

Theodore Roosevelt

preserve

Sierra Club

LEVEL 3

Words to Introduce

naturalist

Sierra Nevada

University of Wisconsin

Yosemite Valley

Theodore Roosevelt

Sierra Club

Sequoia

Mount Rainier

Petrified Forest

Nonfiction Reading Practice, Grade 5 • EMC 3316 • ©2003 by Evan-Moor Corp.

Time Line of John Muir, Father of Our National Parks

April 21, 1838 — Muir born in Scotland.

1849 — Family moves to farm in Wisconsin; works on inventions.

1860 — Muir attends University of Wisconsin.

1867 — Muir is temporarily blinded in factory accident; takes his "thousand mile walk."

1870 — Gives guided tours of Yosemite in Sierra Nevada Mountains.

1890 — Helps establish both Yosemite and Sequoia National Parks.

1892 — Forms the Sierra Club, a conservation organization.

1894 — Publishes his first of many books, *The Mountains of California.*

1901 — Publishes popular book entitled *Our National Parks.*

1903 — President Roosevelt supports Muir's efforts to save millions of acres of forests.

1908 — Muir helps preserve Arizona's Petrified Forest and Grand Canyon.

December 24, 1914 — Muir dies; Muir Woods National Monument named in his honor.

A Biography of John Muir

John Muir was born on April 21, 1838, in Scotland. When John Muir was eleven years old, his family moved to a farm in Wisconsin. Muir's father was very strict. Muir had to work long hours on the farm. He liked to design new inventions in the cellar. Muir invented an early-rising machine. This device was made up of a clock attached to a bed. When it was time to get up, a rod tipped the bed upright, and John was dumped out of bed.

Explorer

John Muir left home in 1860. Muir worked and also attended the University of Wisconsin. He traveled the northern United States and Canada to study plants.

When Muir was 29, he worked in a factory in Indiana. He was fixing a machine with a file. The file flew out of his hand and hit his eye. He went blind. One month later, his vision came back. He decided he would do what he really loved. He quit working at the factory. He began exploring the world and studying nature. On one of his trips, Muir walked 1,000 miles (1,600 km) from Indiana to the Gulf of Mexico. He kept a diary of the plants, animals, and natural wonders he saw.

Naturalist

In 1868, John moved to California. He traveled through Yosemite Valley. John also hiked the Sierra Nevada Mountains. He began to write about nature for magazines and newspapers. People read his stories and came to California to see Yosemite. Muir was a true naturalist. He wanted land, water, and forests to be saved, or preserved. Because of his efforts, Yosemite became a national park in 1890.

John Muir also convinced President Theodore Roosevelt to preserve millions of acres of forests across the West. Muir wrote a number of books about nature. In 1892, John Muir started the Sierra Club. The club worked to protect nature.

John Muir devoted the rest of his life to saving lands in the West. John Muir died on December 24, 1914. A grove of redwood trees were named in his honor. They were called Muir Woods National Monument.

John Muir
1838–1914

Name _____

A Biography of John Muir

Fill in the bubble to answer each question or complete each sentence.

1. As a young boy, John Muir liked to _____.
   - Ⓐ work hard on the farm
   - Ⓑ make new inventions
   - Ⓒ write books
   - Ⓓ walk in the forests

2. After John Muir was injured at his factory job, he decided to _____.
   - Ⓐ work on a different machine
   - Ⓑ go to the University of Wisconsin
   - Ⓒ explore the world and study nature
   - Ⓓ travel immediately to California

3. Because of John Muir's efforts, which area became a national park?
   - Ⓐ Glacier National Park
   - Ⓑ Grand Teton National Park
   - Ⓒ Yellowstone National Park
   - Ⓓ Yosemite National Park

4. John Muir did <u>not</u> _____.
   - Ⓐ work as a sheepherder all his life
   - Ⓑ travel to California
   - Ⓒ write books about nature
   - Ⓓ start the Sierra Club

5. How did people honor John Muir?
   - Ⓐ They named a national park after him.
   - Ⓑ They named a grove of redwood trees after him.
   - Ⓒ They named a university after him.
   - Ⓓ They started the Sierra Club in his honor.

Bonus: John Muir often wrote descriptions in journals of beautiful places he visited. On the back of this page, write a description of a beautiful natural place you have visited.

Father of Our National Parks

John Muir moved to America when he was eleven years old. Muir grew up working long hours on a farm. Whenever he could get away, he wandered into the countryside. That's where his curiosity with the natural world started.

John Muir and Theodore Roosevelt in Yosemite in 1903.

Exploring the World

On one of Muir's first nature trips, he walked 1,000 miles (1,600 km) from Indiana to the Gulf of Mexico. Muir kept a journal of all he saw in nature. Then he sailed to Cuba. Later, he went to Panama. From Panama, Muir sailed up the West Coast to San Francisco. From then on, California was Muir's home.

The Range of Light

In San Francisco, Muir asked the first person he saw where the most beautiful place in California was. That person pointed east to the Sierra Nevada Mountains. Muir walked there and fell in love with the scenery. He saw how the sunlight seemed to light up the mountains with their beauty. Muir later wrote of the Sierras, "They should be called the 'Range of Light'—they are the most beautiful of all the mountain chains I have ever seen."

Father of Our National Parks

In the heart of the Sierra is the Yosemite area. Muir noticed that sheep and cattle were destroying the meadows of Yosemite. He called the animals "hoofed locusts." He brought attention to Yosemite, and that helped make it a national park in 1890. Later, Muir helped create other national parks. He became friends with President Theodore Roosevelt. In 1903, Roosevelt visited Muir in Yosemite. Together, they talked about preserving many of America's natural treasures. Because of that, Muir is called the "Father of our National Parks."

The Sierra Club

Muir's efforts to preserve nature helped start a group called the Sierra Club. The Sierra Club has worked for over one hundred years to preserve special places in nature from being destroyed. One of them was Yosemite National Park. Another was the Grand Canyon. Muir was the club's first president. He said he helped start the club to "make the mountains glad." Muir remained president of the club until he died in 1914.

Name _____

Father of Our National Parks

Fill in the bubble to answer each question or complete each sentence.

1. John Muir was a naturalist. What does it mean to be a *naturalist*?
   - Ⓐ to take care of other people
   - Ⓑ to change the natural world
   - Ⓒ to preserve nature
   - Ⓓ to visit national parks

2. John Muir thought _____ and _____ were destroying the meadows of Yosemite.
   - Ⓐ locusts, sheep
   - Ⓑ locusts, cattle
   - Ⓒ hoofed animals, locusts
   - Ⓓ sheep, cattle

3. Who helped John Muir preserve natural places?
   - Ⓐ President Theodore Roosevelt
   - Ⓑ the Sierra Club
   - Ⓒ both A and B
   - Ⓓ all Californians

4. What mountain range did John Muir call the "Range of Light"?
   - Ⓐ Rocky Mountains
   - Ⓑ Sierra Nevada
   - Ⓒ Yosemite meadows
   - Ⓓ all the mountains in California

5. John Muir became president of _____.
   - Ⓐ the Sierra Club
   - Ⓑ Yosemite
   - Ⓒ the United States
   - Ⓓ the national parks

Bonus: John Muir was called the "Father of our National Parks." On the back of this page, write why you think this is a good name for him.

America's Famous Naturalist

John Muir was one of America's most famous naturalists. As a wilderness explorer, he is known for exciting adventures in California's Sierra Nevada Mountains. He also traveled among Alaska's glaciers, and around the world exploring places of great natural beauty.

So Many Jobs

John Muir had many interests and jobs. He worked on the family farm. Muir worked on inventions that saved time and effort. He worked at a machine shop and took classes at the University of Wisconsin. Muir worked in a sawmill and taught school for a time. Muir was even a sheepherder. John Muir had many interests, but studying plants and nature was his passion.

Muir traveled through the United States and Canada. On one of his trips, Muir walked 1,000 miles (1,600 km) from Indiana to the Gulf of Mexico. He explored natural wonders throughout Europe, Asia, Africa, and the Arctic. He kept a journal, describing the native peoples, plants, animals, and landforms he encountered.

Saving Yosemite

When John Muir was 30 years old, he moved to California. He traveled to California's Yosemite Valley in the Sierra Nevada Mountains. Muir was the first person to explain how the valley was formed by glaciers. He also worked to save Yosemite. Muir wrote articles trying to convince Congress to make Yosemite a national park. Because of his efforts, Yosemite became a national park in 1890.

Preserving Our World

Muir worked with President Theodore Roosevelt to help preserve millions of acres in the West. Muir also founded the Sierra Club. This organization is dedicated to the protection of land, plants, and water. Muir wrote many books about the natural world. Muir's writings helped preserve the areas of Yosemite, Sequoia, Mount Rainier, the Petrified Forest, and the Grand Canyon.

People call John Muir the "Father of our National Parks." Shortly after Muir's death in 1914, the National Park Service was established. The agency protects and manages U.S. national parks. John Muir's work helped Congress realize the need for such an important agency.

John Muir called the Sierras the "Range of Light."

Name _____

America's Famous Naturalist

Fill in the bubble to answer each question or complete each sentence.

1. John Muir is best known for helping preserve, or save, _____.
   - Ⓐ Yosemite
   - Ⓑ the Grand Canyon
   - Ⓒ Mount Rainier
   - Ⓓ the Petrified Forest

2. Which of these groups of words describes saving nature?
   - Ⓐ exploration, encounters, travel
   - Ⓑ preservation, protection, conservation
   - Ⓒ effort, dedication, passion
   - Ⓓ natural beauty, natural wonders, national parks

3. John Muir had all of the following jobs except _____.
   - Ⓐ author of nature books
   - Ⓑ founder of the Sierra Club
   - Ⓒ manager of the National Park Service
   - Ⓓ worker at a machine shop

4. John Muir founded the _____, which was an organization dedicated to _____.
   - Ⓐ the Grand Canyon Club; protecting wildlife
   - Ⓑ the Sierra Club; protecting land, plants, and water
   - Ⓒ the Yosemite National Park Service; protecting the Sierras
   - Ⓓ the U.S. National Park Service; protecting national parks

5. John Muir is called the "Father of our National Parks" because he _____.
   - Ⓐ acted just like his father
   - Ⓑ worked at a national park
   - Ⓒ founded the Sierra Club
   - Ⓓ helped preserve many national parks

Bonus: The Sierra Club remains an active organization today. On the back of this page, write a letter to the national club president telling how you help preserve the world around you. The address is Sierra Club, P.O. Box 52968, Boulder, CO 52968.

Sun Safety

Introducing the Topic

1. Reproduce page 87 for individual students, or make a transparency to use with a group or the whole class.

2. Ask students how many of them like to sunbathe. Tell them that 80 percent of sun exposure occurs before the age of 21. That means children need to be careful when playing in the sun. Too much sun exposure can lead to skin problems later on in life. Show students the chart about sun safety and discuss the rules to follow.

Reading the Selections

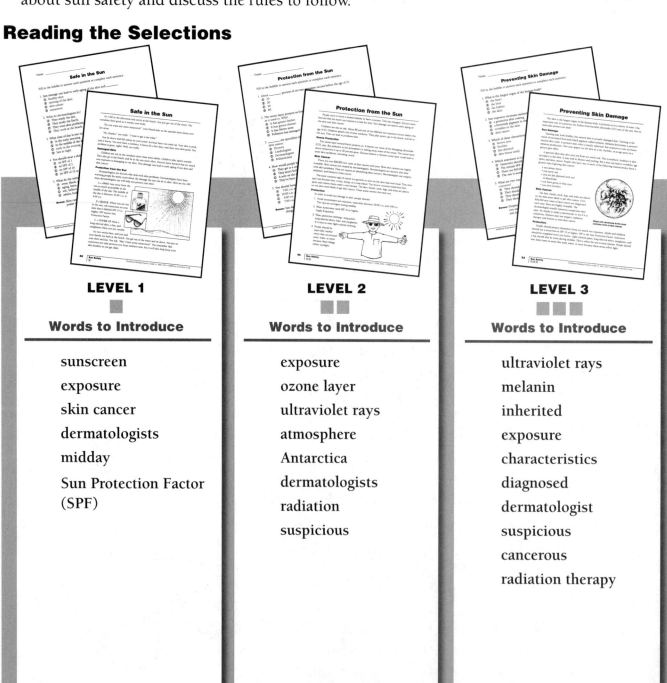

LEVEL 1

Words to Introduce

sunscreen

exposure

skin cancer

dermatologists

midday

Sun Protection Factor
(SPF)

LEVEL 2

Words to Introduce

exposure

ozone layer

ultraviolet rays

atmosphere

Antarctica

dermatologists

radiation

suspicious

LEVEL 3

Words to Introduce

ultraviolet rays

melanin

inherited

exposure

characteristics

diagnosed

dermatologist

suspicious

cancerous

radiation therapy

The Rules for Sun Safety

1. Avoid long periods of direct exposure. Protect yourself during the midday hours. Midday is from 10:00 A.M. to 4:00 P.M. This is when the ultraviolet (UV) radiation is most harmful.

2. Do not sunbathe. Tanned skin is actually damaged skin.

3. Avoid skin damage by using sunscreen. The sunscreen must have a SPF of 15 or higher. SPF stands for Sun Protection Factor. The higher the number, the more the product protects the skin. Apply sunscreen evenly and often.

4. Wear protective light-colored clothing when outdoors. Long pants, a long-sleeved shirt, a hat, and UV-protective sunglasses are recommended.

Safe in the Sun

It's 3:00 in the afternoon and you're at the beach. You just got out of the water. The sunshine feels good as it warms your body.

"Do you want any more sunscreen?" your friend asks as she spreads more lotion over her arms.

"No, thanks," you reply. "I want to get a tan today."

You lie down and fall asleep on your towel. An hour later you wake up. Your skin is pink, and it burns. You now have a sunburn. It hurts for a few days, and then your skin peels. The problem is gone, right? Well, not really.

Damaged Skin

Children are out in the sunshine more than most adults. Children play sports outside. They also go to the beach, and lie in the sun more often. Doctors have learned that too much sun exposure is damaging to our skin. This damage can lead to early aging of our skin and skin cancer.

Protection from the Sun

Dermatologists are doctors who deal with skin problems. Dermatologists have been warning people for many years about the damage the sun can do to skin. Here are the ABC steps dermatologists say will help you protect your skin:

A = AWAY. Stay away from the sun as much as possible in the middle of the day. The middle of the day is between 10:00 A.M. and 4:00 P.M.

B = BLOCK. When you are out in the sun, rub sunscreen on your skin that is labeled SPF 15 or higher. SPF means Sun Protection Factor.

C = COVER UP. Wear a long-sleeved shirt, a hat, and sunglasses when you are outside.

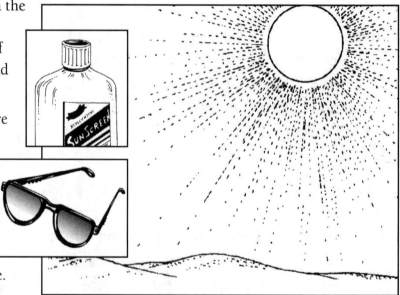

It's two weeks later, and you and your family are back at the beach. You get out of the water and sit down. You put on your shirt and hat. You ask, "May I have some sunscreen?" You remember that sunscreen not only protects you from sunburn now, but it will also help keep your skin healthy as you get older.

Nonfiction Reading Practice, Grade 5 • EMC 3316 • ©2003 by Evan-Moor Corp.

Name _____

Safe in the Sun

Fill in the bubble to answer each question or complete each sentence.

1. Sun damage can lead to early aging of the skin and _____.
   - Ⓐ healthy skin
   - Ⓑ tanning of the skin
   - Ⓒ skin cancer
   - Ⓓ sunscreen

2. What do dermatologists do?
   - Ⓐ They study the sun.
   - Ⓑ They study the Earth.
   - Ⓒ They treat skin problems.
   - Ⓓ They work at the beach.

3. What time of day is sun exposure the worst?
   - Ⓐ in the early morning
   - Ⓑ in the middle of the day
   - Ⓒ early in the evening
   - Ⓓ late at night

4. You should wear a shirt, a hat, sunglasses, and sunscreen with _____.
   - Ⓐ an SPF of 1
   - Ⓑ an SPF of 5
   - Ⓒ an SPF of 10
   - Ⓓ an SPF of 15 or higher

5. What do the initials *ABC* stand for in this article?
   - Ⓐ away, block, cover up
   - Ⓑ aging, burn, cancer
   - Ⓒ ask, believe, control
   - Ⓓ adults, body, children

Bonus: Skin cancer is a serious problem. On the back of this page, design a poster using the ABC steps for sun safety.

Protection from the Sun

People used to think it looked healthy to have a suntan. This has changed. Doctors have learned that too much sun exposure is bad for skin. Sun damage can lead to early aging of the skin and skin cancer.

Children are also at risk. About 80 percent of our lifetime sun exposure occurs before the age of 21. Children spend a lot of time outdoors. They play sports, go to the beach, and lie in the sun. This can lead to problems later.

Ozone Protection

The ozone layer around Earth protects us. It blocks out some of the damaging ultraviolet (UV) rays. But pollution in the atmosphere is taking away some of the ozone. The ozone layer above Antarctica is up to 20 percent gone. Doctors believe a thinner ozone layer could lead to more skin problems, including cancer.

Skin Cancer

There are over 800,000 new cases of skin cancer each year. Most skin cancers are highly treatable. Skin cancers are treated by dermatologists. Dermatologists are doctors who deal with skin problems. They are experts at identifying skin cancers. Dermatologists use surgery, radiation, and lotions to treat cancer.

The most common sign of cancer is a growth or sore on the skin that won't heal. This skin spot can become sore, crusty, lumpy, or it may bleed. The doctor removes suspicious skin spots and checks them under a microscope. The face, hands, neck, legs, and arms are places on the skin most likely to get skin cancer. These areas receive the most sun.

Protection

In order to avoid sun damage to skin, people should:

1. Avoid unnecessary sun exposure, especially between 10:00 A.M. and 4:00 P.M. The rays are strongest during midday.

2. Wear sunscreens rated SPF 15 or higher. Apply frequently.

3. Wear protective clothing—long pants, long-sleeved shirts, hats, and sunglasses. It is best to wear light-colored clothing.

4. People should be especially careful when they are around sand, water, or snow because these things reflect sunlight.

Nonfiction Reading Practice, Grade 5 • EMC 3316 • ©2003 by Evan-Moor Corp.

Name _____

Protection from the Sun

Fill in the bubble to answer each question or complete each sentence.

1. About _____ percent of our sun exposure occurs before the age of 21.
   - Ⓐ 10
   - Ⓑ 20
   - Ⓒ 50
   - Ⓓ 80

2. The ozone layer protects us from the sun's damaging rays, but not as well as it used to. Why?
   - Ⓐ It has gotten thicker.
   - Ⓑ It has gotten thinner.
   - Ⓒ It has blown away.
   - Ⓓ It has gotten colder.

3. _____ are specialists that treat people with skin problems, such as skin cancer.
   - Ⓐ Doctors
   - Ⓑ Cardiologists
   - Ⓒ Dermatologists
   - Ⓓ Pediatricians

4. How would people know if they might have skin cancer?
   - Ⓐ They get to a certain age.
   - Ⓑ They aren't feeling well.
   - Ⓒ A sore on the skin doesn't heal.
   - Ⓓ They've been outside often.

5. You should limit your time outdoors in the sun between _____.
   - Ⓐ 7:00 A.M. and 10:00 A.M.
   - Ⓑ 10:00 A.M. and 4:00 P.M.
   - Ⓒ 3:00 P.M. and 7:00 P.M.
   - Ⓓ 7:00 P.M. and 10:00 P.M.

Bonus: Sun damage is a serious problem. Write a short speech, telling four things people can do to avoid sun damage.

Preventing Skin Damage

The skin is the largest organ of the human body. It protects us in a variety of ways. One important way is it protects our bodies from harmful ultraviolet (UV) rays of the sun. But we must also protect our skin!

Sun Damage

Tanning may look healthy, but tanned skin is actually damaged skin. Tanning is the result of increased brownish-black pigment called melanin. Melanin determines a person's natural skin color. A person's skin color is mostly inherited. But exposure to sun increases melanin production. This may appear on the skin as a tan, freckles, or as age spots as a person gets older.

A person's skin may also turn red from too much sun. This is sunburn. Sunburn is also an injury to the skin. It may lead to blisters and peeling. But it also can lead to wrinkles, age spots, and skin cancer. People who have one or more of the following characteristics have a greater risk of getting skin cancer:

- you always burn
- you never tan
- you are fair-skinned with red or blond hair
- you have green or blue eyes
- you have freckles

Skin Cancer

The face, hands, neck, legs, and arms are places on the skin most likely to get skin cancer. Over 800,000 new cases of skin cancer are diagnosed each year. Most are highly treatable. The dermatologist usually removes a suspicious skin spot. He checks it under a microscope to see if it is cancerous. Doctors may use surgery, radiation therapy, and lotions to treat skin cancer.

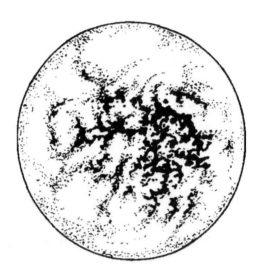

Basal cell carcinoma is the most common form of skin cancer.

Protection

People should protect themselves from too much sun exposure. Adults and children should use a sunscreen at SPF 15 or higher. SPF is the Sun Protection Factor. Sunscreen should be reapplied every two hours. Light-colored pants, long-sleeved shirts, sunglasses, and a hat should also be worn during midday. This is when the sun is most intense. People should also limit times in areas like sand, water, or snow because these areas reflect light.

Name _____

Preventing Skin Damage

Fill in the bubble to answer each question or complete each sentence.

1. What is the largest organ of the human body?
   - Ⓐ the heart
   - Ⓑ the liver
   - Ⓒ the kidney
   - Ⓓ the skin

2. Sun exposure increases melanin production. *Melanin* is _____.
   - Ⓐ a protective skin coating
   - Ⓑ a brownish pigment in the skin
   - Ⓒ wrinkles in the skin
   - Ⓓ skin cancer

3. Which of these characteristics is <u>not</u> likely to be a risk factor for skin cancer?
   - Ⓐ brown eyes
   - Ⓑ freckles
   - Ⓒ fair-skinned
   - Ⓓ skin burns easily

4. Which statement is true?
   - Ⓐ Sunscreen should be applied every five hours.
   - Ⓑ The initials SPF stand for sun, protection, and freckles.
   - Ⓒ There are 800,000 new cases of all types of cancer each year.
   - Ⓓ The sun is most intense during midday.

5. What are two ways people can protect themselves from too much sun exposure?
   - Ⓐ They should dress warm and stay out of the sun.
   - Ⓑ They should dress in light-colored clothes and wear sunscreen.
   - Ⓒ They should wear a hat all the time.
   - Ⓓ They should avoid going anywhere during the day.

Bonus: Despite warnings, people still spend too much time in the sun. Pretend you are a dermatologist. On the back of this page, develop a pamphlet on sun damage and sun protection for your clients.

Bicycle Safety

Introducing the Topic

1. Reproduce page 95 for individual students, or make a transparency to use with a group or the whole class.

2. Ask students what they think is the most important thing they can do to be safe when riding a bicycle. Then share with them that the answer is wearing a helmet. Read and discuss the safety requirements for buying and wearing helmets.

Reading the Selections

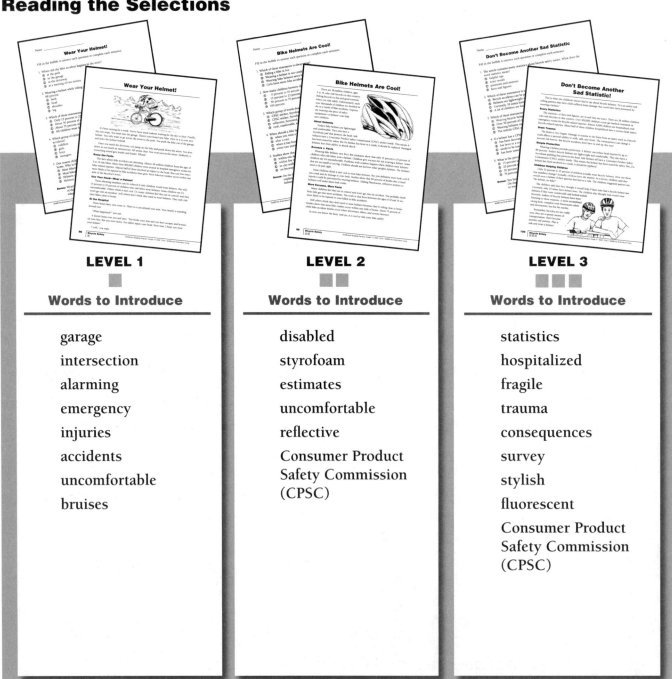

LEVEL 1
Words to Introduce

garage

intersection

alarming

emergency

injuries

accidents

uncomfortable

bruises

LEVEL 2
Words to Introduce

disabled

styrofoam

estimates

uncomfortable

reflective

Consumer Product
Safety Commission
(CPSC)

LEVEL 3
Words to Introduce

statistics

hospitalized

fragile

trauma

consequences

survey

stylish

fluorescent

Consumer Product
Safety Commission
(CPSC)

Bicycle Safety Begins with Wearing the Right Helmet!

- Buy a helmet that has the CPSC (Consumer Product Safety Commission) sticker on it. Remember, not all helmets have this safety seal.

- Try on several helmets before buying one. Buy a helmet that fits your head comfortably and snuggly—not too small or too big. Do not buy a helmet that you can grow into. It should fit you right now. Do not use other family members' or friends' helmets.

- Your helmet should sit level on your head—not tilted forward, backward, or sideways. Remember not to wear a hat under your helmet.

- Your helmet should have strong, wide straps. It should be fastened at all times when riding your bicycle.

- Your helmet should be replaced when you have outgrown it. The set of foam pads that are on the inside may be changed also so the helmet will still fit properly. Your helmet should be replaced right away if it has been damaged.

Wear Your Helmet!

It's been raining for a week. You've been stuck indoors waiting for the sky to clear. Finally, the rain stops. You dash into the garage. There's your brand new bike. Next to it is your new helmet. You only want to go across the street to the park. You push the bike out of the garage and leave the helmet behind.

Once you reach the driveway, you jump on the bike and pedal down the street. You slow down as you reach an intersection. All seems clear. You zoom across the street. Suddenly, a screeching sound gets louder and louder. Wham!

Know the Facts

The facts about bike accidents are alarming. Almost 28 million children from the ages of 5 to 14 ride bikes. More than 300,000 children a year are treated in hospital emergency rooms for bike-related injuries. Almost half of these involved an injury to the head. Boys are five times more likely to be injured in bike accidents than girls. Most bike/car crashes occur within one mile of the bicyclist's home.

Use Your Head—Wear a Helmet!

These alarming numbers can be reduced if only children would wear helmets. But only 15 to 25 percent of children who ride bikes wear helmets. Some children say it's uncomfortable. Others think it isn't cool. Or, many children feel they are in control, and they won't get into an accident. Still others don't think they need to wear helmets. They only ride their bikes close to home.

At the Hospital

Three hours later, you come to. There is a cast around your arm. Your family is standing around you.

"What happened?" you ask.

A doctor leans over you and says, "You broke your arm and you have scrapes and bruises on your face. But you were lucky. You didn't injure your head. Next time, I hope you wear your helmet."

"I will," you reply.

Name _____

Wear Your Helmet!

Fill in the bubble to answer each question or complete each sentence.

1. Where did the bike accident happen in the story?
   - Ⓐ at the park
   - Ⓑ in the garage
   - Ⓒ in the driveway
   - Ⓓ at a meeting of two streets

2. Wearing a helmet while riding a bike can reduce _____ injuries dramatically.
   - Ⓐ back
   - Ⓑ head
   - Ⓒ shoulder
   - Ⓓ leg

3. Which of these statements is true?
   - Ⓐ Only 15 to 25 percent of children wear helmets.
   - Ⓑ About 50 percent of children wear helmets.
   - Ⓒ About 75 percent of children wear helmets.
   - Ⓓ All children wear bike helmets.

4. Which group of children is five times more likely to be injured in bike accidents?
   - Ⓐ toddlers
   - Ⓑ girls
   - Ⓒ boys
   - Ⓓ teenagers

5. One reason children give for not wearing a helmet is that they ride close to home. Why is this not a good excuse?
   - Ⓐ Most bike/car crashes occur within one mile of the bicyclist's home.
   - Ⓑ Most bike/car crashes occur near a school.
   - Ⓒ Helmets can look cool.
   - Ⓓ Helmets can be comfortable.

Bonus: Wearing a helmet while riding a bike is a serious concern. On the back of this page, design a poster that will get more children to use a helmet when riding a bike!

Bike Helmets Are Cool!

There are 28 million children, ages 5 to 14, who ride bicycles in this country. Riding bicycles is fun and good exercise when you ride safely. Unfortunately, each year thousands of children are disabled or die as a result of bike accidents. Experts say wearing one piece of safety equipment—a helmet—can help save children.

About Helmets

Today's bike helmets are lightweight and comfortable. They also have a Styrofoam pad that protects the head. Safe helmets have a Consumer Product Safety Commission (CPSC) sticker inside. This means it has been tested for safety. But if a helmet has been in a crash, it should be replaced. Damaged helmets lose their ability to absorb shock.

Excuses v. Facts

Wearing bike helmets save lives. But estimates show that only 15 to 25 percent of children who ride bikes wear a helmet. Children give excuses for not wearing a helmet. Some children say it's uncomfortable. Problems with comfort happen when children wear helmets that are too small or too big. Children should not borrow other people's helmets. The helmets need to fit just right.

Some children think it isn't cool to wear bike helmets. But you definitely won't look cool if you crash and do damage to your body. Studies show that 90 percent of deaths due to head injuries could be prevented by wearing helmets. Adding fluorescent, reflective stickers to helmets will make them look cooler.

More Excuses, More Facts

Many children feel they are in control and won't get into an accident. You probably think little kids get into more accidents. The truth is that boys between the ages of 10 and 14 are more likely to be injured or even killed in bike accidents.

Still others think they don't need to wear helmets because they're riding close to home. Studies show that most bike crashes occur within one mile of home. About 75 percent of child bike-accident deaths occur where driveways, alleys, and streets intersect.

So now you know the facts. And yes, it *is* cool to ride your bike safely!

Name _____

Bike Helmets Are Cool!

Fill in the bubble to answer each question or complete each sentence.

1. Which of these statements is always true?
   - Ⓐ Riding a bike is fun.
   - Ⓑ Wearing a helmet is not comfortable.
   - Ⓒ Wearing bike helmets saves lives.
   - Ⓓ Girls have more bike accidents than boys.

2. How many children between the ages of 5 and 14 wear bike helmets?
   - Ⓐ 0 to 10 percent
   - Ⓑ 15 to 25 percent
   - Ⓒ 50 to 75 percent
   - Ⓓ 100 percent

3. Which group of words describes a safe bike helmet?
   - Ⓐ CPSC sticker, Styrofoam pad, and heavy
   - Ⓑ CPSC sticker, Styrofoam pad, and lightweight
   - Ⓒ reflective, borrowed, stylish
   - Ⓓ cool, comfortable, and big

4. When should a bike helmet be replaced?
   - Ⓐ when you want a new one
   - Ⓑ after a rain
   - Ⓒ when it has been in a crash
   - Ⓓ every two years

5. Studies show that most bike accidents happen _____ and _____.
   - Ⓐ within one mile of home, at intersections
   - Ⓑ within five miles of home, at intersections
   - Ⓒ in city traffic, near buses
   - Ⓓ on freeways, at on-ramps

Bonus: On the back of this page, write an article for your school newspaper explaining why wearing bike helmets is cool. Add a picture of a cool helmet!

Don't Become Another Sad Statistic!

This is what one children's doctor had to say about bicycle helmets: "It is an awful task telling parents that their child suffered brain damage that could have been prevented by wearing a helmet."

Scary Statistics

The statistics, or facts and figures, are in and they are scary. There are 28 million children who ride bicycles in this country. Over 300,000 children a year get medical treatment in emergency rooms for bicycle-related injuries. Almost 9,000 children are hospitalized with bicycle-related injuries. About half of those children hospitalized have a serious head injury.

Brain Trauma

The brain is very fragile. Damage or trauma to the brain from an injury such as a bicycle crash affects a person's ability to walk, talk, and think. The consequences can change a person's life forever. But bicycle accidents don't have to end up this way!

Simple Protection

Wearing a helmet provides protection. A helmet can reduce head injuries by up to 88 percent. Today's bicycle helmets are lightweight and comfortable. They also have a Styrofoam padding that protects the head. Safe helmets all have a Consumer Product Safety Commission (CPSC) sticker inside. This means the helmet has been tested for safety. But, if a helmet has been involved in a crash, it should be replaced.

Children Helping Children

Only 15 to 25 percent of children actually wear bicycle helmets. How can these low numbers change? Actually, children have the answer. In a survey, children said they would wear a helmet if their parents had that as a rule. The children suggested parents say, "No helmet, no bike!"

The children said that they thought it would help if their state had a bicycle helmet law. Currently, only 19 states have helmet laws. The children also thought kids would wear helmets if they were comfortable and looked stylish. Recently, makers of bicycle helmets have been listening to these requests. A more streamlined racing look, complete with fluorescent colors and decorations, has hit the market.

Remember, bicycles are not really toys; they are a speedy means of transportation. Don't become another sad statistic. Play it safe and wear a helmet!

Nonfiction Reading Practice, Grade 5 • EMC 3316 • ©2003 by Evan-Moor Corp.

Name _____

Don't Become Another Sad Statistic

Fill in the bubble to answer each question or complete each sentence.

1. The article contains many statistics about bicycle safety issues. What does the word *statistics* mean?
   - Ⓐ helpful tips
   - Ⓑ scary words
   - Ⓒ questions and answers
   - Ⓓ facts and figures

2. Which of these statements is a *statistic*?
   - Ⓐ Bicycle accidents can be prevented.
   - Ⓑ Helmets are lightweight and comfortable.
   - Ⓒ Currently, 19 states have helmet laws.
   - Ⓓ A lot of children are hospitalized with bicycle-related injuries.

3. Which of these statements is false?
   - Ⓐ Wearing bicycle helmets saves lives.
   - Ⓑ Over 50 percent of children wear bicycle helmets all the time.
   - Ⓒ Wearing helmets can reduce head injuries by up to 88 percent.
   - Ⓓ The initials CPSC stand for Consumer Product Safety Commission.

4. If a helmet has a CPSC sticker inside it, this means it _____.
   - Ⓐ has been decorated by a child
   - Ⓑ has been in a crash
   - Ⓒ needs to be tested for safety
   - Ⓓ has been tested for safety

5. What is the percentage range of children who wear bicycle helmets?
   - Ⓐ 15 to 25 percent
   - Ⓑ 25 to 50 percent
   - Ⓒ 50 to 75 percent
   - Ⓓ 75 to 100 percent

Bonus: You have been asked to give a speech to your class on bicycle safety. On the back of this page, write a speech that will convince your friends to wear helmets. Be sure to include at least four statistics.

Mark Wellman

Introducing the Topic

1. Reproduce page 103 for individual students, or make a transparency to use with a group or the whole class.

2. Show students the picture of Mark Wellman. Tell students that Wellman is an expert mountain climber who also happens to be disabled. Also point out the special equipment he and others designed for disabled athletes.

Reading the Selections

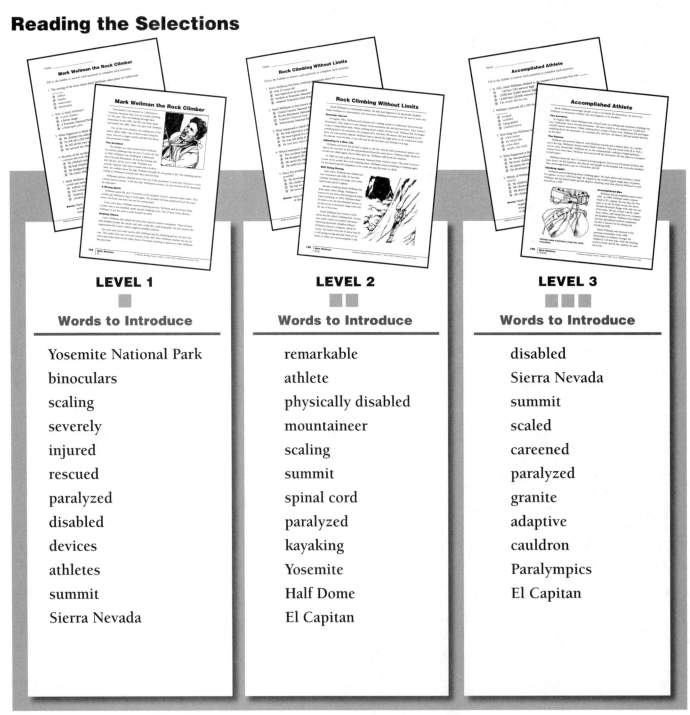

LEVEL 1

Words to Introduce

Yosemite National Park

binoculars

scaling

severely

injured

rescued

paralyzed

disabled

devices

athletes

summit

Sierra Nevada

LEVEL 2

Words to Introduce

remarkable

athlete

physically disabled

mountaineer

scaling

summit

spinal cord

paralyzed

kayaking

Yosemite

Half Dome

El Capitan

LEVEL 3

Words to Introduce

disabled

Sierra Nevada

summit

scaled

careened

paralyzed

granite

adaptive

cauldron

Paralympics

El Capitan

Mark Wellman, Mountain Climber

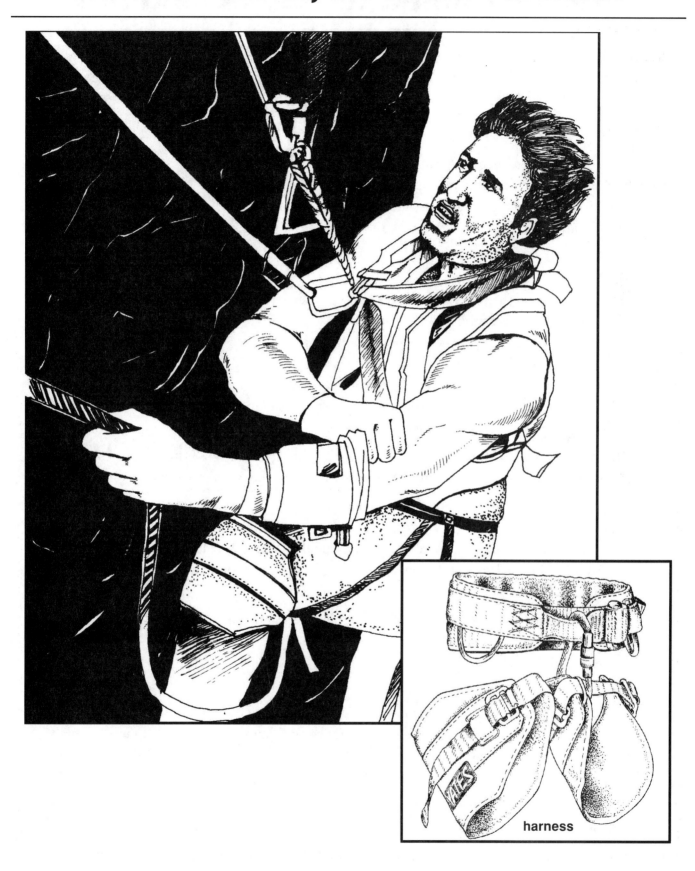

harness

Mark Wellman the Rock Climber

Your family is on vacation in California at Yosemite National Park. You see people standing by the road. They are looking through their binoculars at the cliffs. You lift your binoculars and search the cliffs. There you spot rock climbers.

Two of the rock climbers are scaling one of the park's tallest cliffs. One of them is just using his arms. You see a ranger nearby and ask him about this mountain climber.

The Accident

The climber is a man named Mark Wellman. He started climbing when he was 12 years old. But in 1982, Wellman was climbing in California's Sierra Nevada Mountains. He lost his footing and fell 100 feet (30 m) over a cliff. Wellman was severely injured, with open wounds and a broken back. He couldn't move his legs. Wellman thought he was going to die. His climbing partner tended to Wellman's wounds and then went for help.

Wellman's partner climbed down the rest of the mountain. It took him 19 hours to reach a forest service station. A full day after Wellman's accident, he was rescued off the mountain by helicopter.

A Strong Spirit

Wellman spent the next $7\frac{1}{2}$ months in the hospital. Doctors operated many times. They couldn't get Wellman's legs to work again. The accident left him paralyzed from the waist down. His body was hurt, but not his strong spirit.

A few years later, Wellman started climbing again. Wellman and his friend, Mike Corbet, who is not disabled, made special climbing tools. One of these tools allowed Wellman to use his arms to pull himself up cliffs.

Helping Others

Later, Wellman also helped develop other special outdoor equipment. These devices help disabled people ski, kayak, sail, surf, scuba dive, and hang-glide. He also started the organization No Limits, which supports disabled athletes.

You turn your eyes back up the cliff. Wellman and his climbing partner are near the top. They make their way over the summit of the cliff. After Wellman reaches the top, he turns and looks down at the valley below. Everyone watching is amazed at what Wellman has just done.

Nonfiction Reading Practice, Grade 5 • EMC 3316 • ©2003 by Evan-Moor Corp.

Name _____

Mark Wellman the Rock Climber

Fill in the bubble to answer each question or complete each sentence.

1. The setting of the story about Mark Wellman takes place in California's _____.
   - Ⓐ valleys
   - Ⓑ forests
   - Ⓒ waterways
   - Ⓓ mountains

2. Who is Mark Wellman?
   - Ⓐ a rock climber
   - Ⓑ a forest ranger
   - Ⓒ a Yosemite National Park worker
   - Ⓓ a helicopter pilot

3. What happened to Mark Wellman in 1982?
   - Ⓐ He climbed the tallest mountain in the United States.
   - Ⓑ He fell off a cliff while rock climbing.
   - Ⓒ He fell all the way to the bottom of a mountain.
   - Ⓓ He rescued his climbing partner off a mountain.

4. Because of the accident, Mark Wellman became disabled. How was he able to continue his rock climbing?
   - Ⓐ He climbed only smaller hills.
   - Ⓑ He had climbing partners carry him up mountains.
   - Ⓒ He designed special climbing tools to help him climb.
   - Ⓓ He wasn't able to continue climbing.

5. Mark Wellman scaled to the summit of many mountains. What do the words *scaled* and *summit* mean as used in this article?
   - Ⓐ walked, iciest part
   - Ⓑ fell, bottom
   - Ⓒ climbed, cliff
   - Ⓓ climbed, top

Bonus: Mark Wellman did not give up after he became disabled. Write a newspaper story about Mark Wellman and his remarkable ability to succeed.

Rock Climbing Without Limits

Mark Wellman is a remarkable athlete. He also just happens to be physically disabled. Mark Wellman is a mountaineer who has been climbing mountains since he was 12 years old.

Severely Injured

In August 1982, Wellman and a friend were scaling a peak in California's Sierra Nevada Mountains. They made it to the summit of the mountain late and hurried down. They wanted to get to camp before dark. While rushing down a slope of loose rock, Wellman fell. He began tumbling down the mountain. He dropped off a 100-foot (30-meter) cliff and landed on his back. He was severely injured. Wellman had to spend the night alone in the wilderness while his partner went for help. It was cold and he did not have any feeling in his legs.

Adjusting to a New Life

Wellman survived, but he had to adjust to the fact that he had a permanent spinal cord injury. He was only in his 30s and paralyzed from the waist down. Wellman didn't think he would ever climb again. But he didn't give up. Wellman still loved the outdoors.

In 1986, he took a job at the Yosemite National Park visitor's center. This park is known as one of the world's best rock climbing areas. Wellman started thinking of climbing again. He developed special equipment so he could use just his arms to climb.

Still Going Strong

Since then, Wellman has climbed all over Yosemite's tall cliffs. He has also climbed Yosemite's two large rock walls, Half Dome and El Capitan.

Besides climbing, Mark Wellman has done many other things. Wellman is known for his downhill skiing and white-water kayaking. In 1993, Wellman skied 50 miles to be the first disabled person to sit-ski across a mountain range with only the use of his arms.

Mark Wellman has written a book about his life entitled *Climbing Back*. He has also made videos on outdoor adventure featuring physically disabled athletes. Wellman started a company called No Limits. He wants everyone to know that he is still going strong and that there are no limits to what you can accomplish in life.

Nonfiction Reading Practice, Grade 5 • EMC 3316 • ©2003 by Evan-Moor Corp.

Name _____

Rock Climbing Without Limits

Fill in the bubble to answer each question or complete each sentence.

1. Mark Wellman has been climbing mountains since he _____.
   - Ⓐ was 12 years old
   - Ⓑ was injured in an accident
   - Ⓒ worked at Yosemite National Park
   - Ⓓ climbed Yosemite's Half Dome

2. Mark Wellman is best known for climbing the mountains in _____.
   - Ⓐ Grand Canyon National Park
   - Ⓑ Rocky Mountain National Park
   - Ⓒ Yosemite National Park
   - Ⓓ Yellowstone National Park

3. What happened to Mark Wellman that left him paralyzed?
   - Ⓐ He was injured in a skiing accident.
   - Ⓑ He was injured in a rock climbing accident.
   - Ⓒ He was left alone in the wilderness.
   - Ⓓ He was hurt when he was 12 years old.

4. Which statement is not true about Wellman's rock climbing accident?
   - Ⓐ The accident happened as he was reaching the summit.
   - Ⓑ He dropped off a 100-foot (30-meter) cliff.
   - Ⓒ He spent the night alone in the wilderness.
   - Ⓓ He suffered a spinal cord injury.

5. Since his accident, Mark Wellman has continued to climb. How is that possible?
   - Ⓐ He loves the outdoors.
   - Ⓑ He climbs only smaller mountains now.
   - Ⓒ He has his partners carry him.
   - Ⓓ He developed special tools to help him.

Bonus: Since Mark Wellman's accident, he has accomplished a lot. On the back of this page, make a list of at least six things he has done since 1982.

Accomplished Athlete

Mark Wellman encourages people to not set limits for themselves. He never has. Wellman is a mountain climber who also happens to be disabled.

The Accident

In August 1982, Mark Wellman and a friend went on a hiking and rock climbing trip into California's Sierra Nevada Mountains. The men scaled to the summit of a 13,000-foot (20,800-meter) mountain. While rushing down a slope of loose rock, Wellman fell and began tumbling down the mountain. He careened off a 100-foot (30-meter) cliff and landed directly on his back.

The Rescue

Wellman was severely injured, with bleeding wounds and a broken back. He couldn't move his legs. Wellman's friend tended to Mark's injuries. Then his friend took off to find a rescue team. Meanwhile, Wellman lay on the mountainside, waiting in frigid darkness. Twenty-four hours later, Wellman was rescued off the mountain. He was taken to a hospital by helicopter.

Wellman spent the next $7\frac{1}{2}$ months having surgeries, but he was left paralyzed from the waist down. He felt hopeless. But then he met people in the hospital who were also disabled. They encouraged him to go on, wheelchair and all.

Climbing Again

Wellman started thinking about climbing again. He made plans with a friend to climb El Capitan. At over 3,000 feet high, El Capitan is the world's largest single piece of granite. Wellman and his friend made special adaptive climbing tools that allowed Wellman to pull himself up a cliff.

Accomplished Man

Wellman has accomplished much since 1982. In 1996, Wellman made a repeat climb of El Capitan. He was also the first man to sit-ski 50 miles across the Sierra Nevada Mountain Range with only the use of his arms. He has written a book, made three videos, and started his own company for disabled athletes. Wellman also helped develop specialized outdoor equipment. He also is known for his skiing and kayaking skills.

Mark Wellman was honored at the opening ceremonies of the 1996 Paralympics in Atlanta, Georgia. He climbed a 120-foot rope, with the flaming torch in hand, and lit the cauldron to start the event.

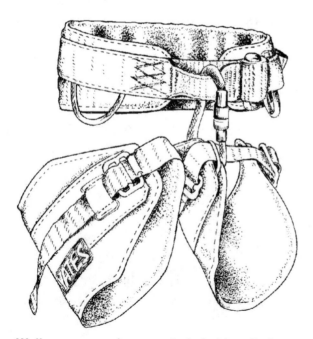

Wellman uses a harness to help him climb mountains.

Nonfiction Reading Practice, Grade 5 • EMC 3316 • ©2003 by Evan-Moor Corp.

Name _____

Accomplished Athlete

Fill in the bubble to answer each question or complete each sentence.

1. In 1982, Mark Wellman climbed to the summit of a mountain that was _____.
   - Ⓐ   120 feet (192 meters) high
   - Ⓑ   3,000 feet (4,800 meters) high
   - Ⓒ   13,000 feet (20,800 meters) high
   - Ⓓ   The article did not say.

2. Wellman careened off a 100-foot (30-meter) cliff. The word *careened* means _____.
   - Ⓐ jumped
   - Ⓑ tumbled
   - Ⓒ hang-glided
   - Ⓓ climbed down

3. How long was Wellman stuck in the wilderness waiting to be rescued?
   - Ⓐ a few hours
   - Ⓑ nearly one week
   - Ⓒ a few days
   - Ⓓ an entire day

4. What happened to Mark Wellman as a result of the rock climbing accident?
   - Ⓐ He was paralyzed from the waist down, but continued to climb.
   - Ⓑ He never climbed the Sierra Nevada Mountains again.
   - Ⓒ He spent the rest of his life in a hospital.
   - Ⓓ He developed special tools, but never used them himself.

5. Which of Wellman's athletic accomplishments was <u>not</u> mentioned in this article?
   - Ⓐ He climbed El Capitan in Yosemite.
   - Ⓑ He climbed Half Dome in Yosemite.
   - Ⓒ He skied 50 miles with only the use of his arms.
   - Ⓓ He climbed a 120-foot rope at the Paralympics in Atlanta, Georgia.

Bonus: Mark Wellman visits schools and talks about how people can turn a negative experience into a positive one. He says that everyone can be a winner. On the back of this page, write three questions you would want to ask Mark Wellman if he came to your school.

Batting Averages

Introducing the Topic

1. Reproduce page 111 for individual students, or make a transparency to use with a group or the whole class.

2. There are a lot of vocabulary words and terms to know in baseball. Show students the chart of baseball words and terms to familiarize them with the terminology. Then look at Barry Bonds' statistics. Tell students they are about to learn how to find the batting average for baseball players.

Reading the Selections

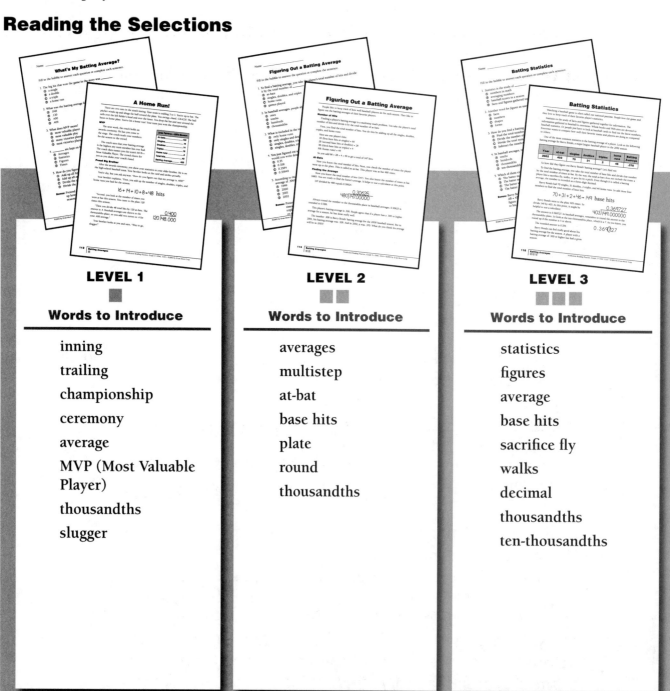

LEVEL 1
Words to Introduce

inning

trailing

championship

ceremony

average

MVP (Most Valuable Player)

thousandths

slugger

LEVEL 2
Words to Introduce

averages

multistep

at-bat

base hits

plate

round

thousandths

LEVEL 3
Words to Introduce

statistics

figures

average

base hits

sacrifice fly

walks

decimal

thousandths

ten-thousandths

Learning the Language of Baseball Statistics

G = Games played

AB = At-bat or the number of times the player comes up to bat

H = Number of hits by a player that resulted in getting on base

1B = First-base hit or a single

2B = Second-base hit or a double

3B = Third-base hit or a triple

HR = Home run

BA = Batting average

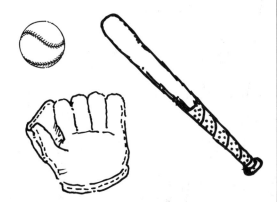

#25 Barry Bonds
San Francisco Giants
2002 Season Statistics

G	AB	H	1B	2B	3B	HR	BA
143	403	149	70	31	2	46	0.370

If a player has a batting average of 0.300 or higher, he has had a great season. Barry Bonds had a fantastic 2002 baseball season. He was voted the National League's MVP (Most Valuable Player).

A Home Run!

There are two outs in the ninth inning. Your team is trailing 3 to 1. You're up to bat. The pitcher winds up and slings the ball toward the plate. You swing—hard. CRACK! The ball sails over the left fielder's head and over the fence. You drop the bat and race around the bases to home plate. You've hit a home run! Your team just won the championship!

MVP

The next week, the coach holds an awards ceremony. He has you come to the stage. The coach reads your numbers for the season to the crowd.

Jose Ramirez—2002 Season	
At-bats	120
Singles	16
Doubles	14
Triples	10
Home runs	8
Total hits	48
Batting Average	.400

The coach says that your batting average is the highest any team member has ever had. The coach then names you the team's MVP—Most Valuable Player. The crowd cheers for you as you shake your coach's hand.

Proud Big Brother

After the awards ceremony, you show your statistics to your older brother. He is on the high school baseball team. Your brother looks at the card and smiles proudly.

You're shy, but you ask anyway. "How do you figure out that my average is .400?"

Your brother explains, "First, you add up the number of singles, doubles, triples, and home runs you had for the season.

$$16 + 14 + 10 + 8 = 48 \text{ hits}$$

"Second, you look at the number of times you were at-bat this season. You came to the plate 120 times this season.

"Then you divide 48 total hits by 120 at-bats. The answer is .4. Baseball averages are shown to the thousandths place, so you add two zeroes to .4 for your .400 average."

$$120 \overline{)48.000} \quad 0.400$$

Your brother looks at you and says, "Way to go, slugger!"

Name _____

A Home Run!

Fill in the bubble to answer each question or complete each sentence.

1. The big hit that won the game in the story was _____.
   - Ⓐ a single
   - Ⓑ a double
   - Ⓒ a triple
   - Ⓓ a home run

2. What was the batting average for the person in the article?
   - Ⓐ .048
   - Ⓑ .120
   - Ⓒ .400
   - Ⓓ .406

3. What does *MVP* mean?
   - Ⓐ most valuable player
   - Ⓑ most valuable play
   - Ⓒ many victories played
   - Ⓓ most victories played

4. _____ are kept on baseball players. These are all the facts and numbers.
   - Ⓐ Averages
   - Ⓑ Statistics
   - Ⓒ Figures
   - Ⓓ Times

5. How do you figure out a batting average?
   - Ⓐ Add up all hits.
   - Ⓑ Add up all at-bats.
   - Ⓒ Divide the total number of hits by the number of times at-bat.
   - Ⓓ Divide the number of times at-bat by the total number of hits.

Bonus: Pretend you have just been named MVP. On the back of this page, add up how many singles, doubles, triples, and home runs you had for the season.

Figuring Out a Batting Average

People like to keep track of how well baseball players do each season. They like to figure out the batting averages of their favorite players.

Number of Hits

Finding a player's batting average is a multistep math problem. You take the player's total number of hits and divide it by the total number of at-bats.

First, you find the total number of hits. You do this by adding up all the singles, doubles, triples, and home runs.

> ### Here are one player's hits:
> 1B (first-base hits or singles) = 66
> 2B (second-base hits or doubles) = 28
> 3B (third-base hits or triples) = 4
> HR (home runs) = 49
>
> So you add 66 + 28 + 4 + 49 to get a total of 147 hits.

At-Bats

Now you know the total number of hits. Next, you check the number of times the player went up to the plate. This is called an at-bat. This player was at-bat 480 times.

Finding the Average

Now you know the total number of hits (147). You also know the number of times at-bat (480). You are ready to find the batter's average. It helps to use a calculator at this point.

147 divided by 480 equals 0.30625.

$$480 \overline{)147.00000} = 0.30625$$

Always round the number to the thousandths place in baseball averages. When rounded, 0.30625 is 0.306.

This player's batting average is .306. People agree that if a player has a .300 or higher average for a season, he has done really well.

The number .306 is Barry Bonds' batting average for the 2000 baseball season. But in 2001, his batting average was .328. And in 2002, it was .370. What do you think his average will be in 2003?

Name _____

Figuring Out a Batting Average

Fill in the bubble to answer the question or complete the sentence.

1. To find a batting average, you take the player's total number of hits and divide it by the total number of _____.
   Ⓐ at-bats
   Ⓑ singles, doubles, and triples
   Ⓒ home runs
   Ⓓ games played

2. In baseball averages, people always round the number to the _____ place.
   Ⓐ ones
   Ⓑ tenths
   Ⓒ hundreds
   Ⓓ thousandths

3. What is included in the total number of hits?
   Ⓐ only home runs
   Ⓑ only singles and doubles
   Ⓒ singles, doubles, triples, and home runs
   Ⓓ singles, doubles, triples, home runs, and walks

4. You just figured out a player's batting average to be 0.35842. What number would you write down as the player's batting average?
   Ⓐ .35
   Ⓑ .358
   Ⓒ .3584
   Ⓓ .35849

5. According to this article, in which season did Barry Bonds have a batting average of .306?
   Ⓐ 1999
   Ⓑ 2000
   Ⓒ 2001
   Ⓓ 2002

Bonus: Pretend you are a major league baseball player. You have been at-bat 72 times this season. Make a card that shows how many singles, doubles, triples, and home runs you have hit. Also, include your batting average on the card.

Batting Statistics

Watching a baseball game is often called our national pastime. People love the game and they love to keep track of their favorite player's statistics.

Statistics is the study of facts and figures gathered together for information. The information gathered in baseball is enormous. Whole books and Web sites are devoted to baseball statistics. Or people just have to look at baseball cards to find out the latest numbers. Everyone wants to compare how well their favorite teams and players are doing as compared to others.

One of the most common statistics is the batting average of a player. Look at the following 2002 season batting average for Barry Bonds, a major league baseball player.

Year	at-bat	singles	doubles	triples	home runs	Batting Average
2002	403	70	31	2	46	.370

So how did they figure out Barry Bonds' batting average? Let's find out.

To find the batting average, you take the total number of base hits and divide that number by the total number of times at-bat. By the way, the total at-bats does not include the times a player hits a sacrifice fly, walks, or gets hit by a pitch. Even though it is called a batting average, the number is recorded as a three-digit decimal.

Barry Bonds had 70 singles, 31 doubles, 2 triples, and 46 home runs. So add those four numbers to find the total number of base hits.

$$70 + 31 + 2 + 46 = 149 \text{ base hits}$$

Barry Bonds went to the plate 403 times. So divide 149 by 403. At this point, it might be helpful to use a calculator.

$$403 \overline{)149.000000} = 0.369727$$

The answer is 0.369727. In baseball averages, remember to round the answer to the thousandths place. So look at the ten-thousandths place, which is a 7. As you know, you round up if the number is 5 or above.

The rounded answer is 0.370. $0.369\textcircled{7}27$

Barry Bonds can feel really good about his batting average for the season. A player with a batting average of .300 or higher has had a great season.

Batting Statistics

Fill in the bubble to answer each question or complete each sentence.

1. *Statistics* is the study of _____.
   - Ⓐ numbers in math
   - Ⓑ averaging numbers
   - Ⓒ baseball scores in a season
   - Ⓓ facts and figures gathered together for information

2. Another word for *figures* as used in statistics is _____.
   - Ⓐ facts
   - Ⓑ numbers
   - Ⓒ shapes
   - Ⓓ forms

3. How do you find a batting average?
   - Ⓐ Find the total number of base hits.
   - Ⓑ Divide the number of home runs by the number of times at-bat.
   - Ⓒ Divide the total number of base hits by the number of times at-bat.
   - Ⓓ Subtract the number of base hits from the number of times at-bat.

4. In baseball averages, remember to round the answer to the _____ place.
   - Ⓐ tenths
   - Ⓑ hundreds
   - Ⓒ thousandths
   - Ⓓ ten-thousandths

5. Which of these events is always used to find the batting average?
   - Ⓐ The batter hits a home run.
   - Ⓑ The batter hits a sacrifice fly.
   - Ⓒ The batter walks to first base.
   - Ⓓ The batter gets hit by a pitch.

Bonus: Barry Bonds had a great 2001 season. Here are his statistics: AB = 476, 1B = 49, 2B = 32, 3B = 2, HR = 73. On the back of this page, figure out the batting average for Barry Bonds' 2001 season. Compare it to his 2002 season and decide which year was his best.

Global Warming

Introducing the Topic

1. Reproduce page 119 for individual students, or make a transparency to use with a group or the whole class.

2. Ask students if they know what the term *global warming* means. Tell students the definition is a continuing temperature increase in Earth's surface. Ask students for possible causes of this warming trend. Then show students the illustration of possible causes of global warming. Show students the graph of the Earth's average surface temperatures. Point out how they are increasing.

Reading the Selections

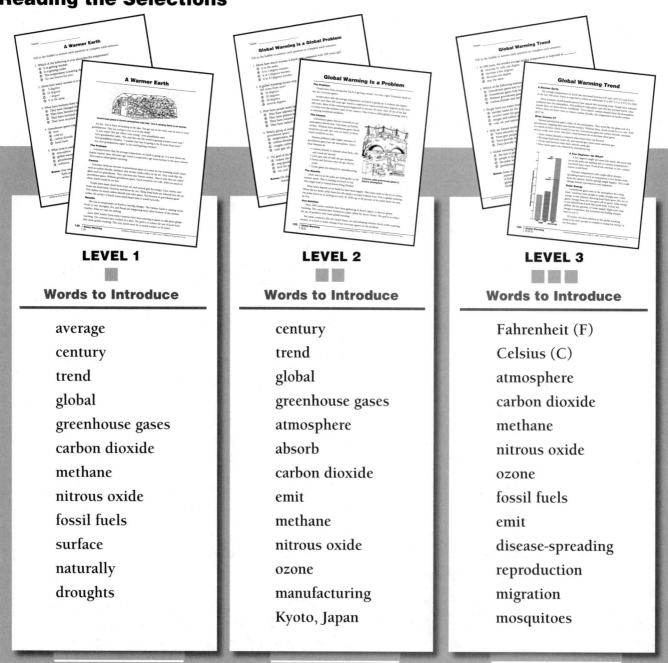

LEVEL 1
Words to Introduce

average

century

trend

global

greenhouse gases

carbon dioxide

methane

nitrous oxide

fossil fuels

surface

naturally

droughts

LEVEL 2
Words to Introduce

century

trend

global

greenhouse gases

atmosphere

absorb

carbon dioxide

emit

methane

nitrous oxide

ozone

manufacturing

Kyoto, Japan

LEVEL 3
Words to Introduce

Fahrenheit (F)

Celsius (C)

atmosphere

carbon dioxide

methane

nitrous oxide

ozone

fossil fuels

emit

disease-spreading

reproduction

migration

mosquitoes

Earth's Warming Temperatures

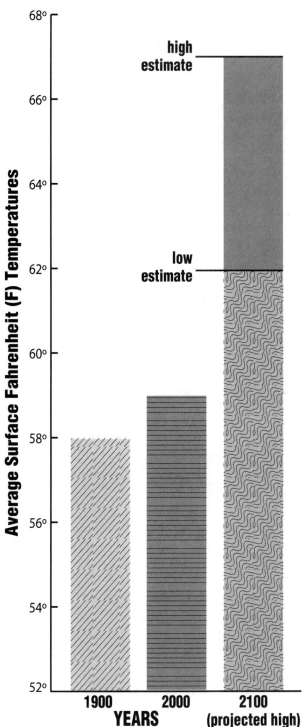

Average Surface Fahrenheit (F) Temperatures

high estimate

low estimate

68°

66°

64°

62°

60°

58°

56°

54°

52°

YEARS

1900   2000   2100 (projected high)

In the last 100 years, Earth's surface temperature has increased by one degree F. What kind of increase in temperature is expected in another 100 years?

Possible Causes of Global Warming

Carbon Dioxide   Nitrous Oxide

Methane

Ozone • Ozone • Ozone • Ozone • Ozone

When people pollute Earth, too many greenhouse gases are released into the atmosphere. An increase in greenhouse gases causes the temperature of Earth to rise.

A Warmer Earth

Greenhouse gases in Earth's atmosphere trap heat. This is causing Earth to be warmer.

It's hot. You've been swimming in the lake. You get out of the water and sit next to your grandparents. They are trying to stay cool in the shade.

"It sure wasn't this hot when I was young," your grandfather says.

Your grandmother adds, "Yes, and they say the world is getting warmer every year."

Your grandfather finishes. "I wonder how hot it's going to be 50 years from now?"

Are your grandparents right? Is the world getting warmer?

The Problem

Scientists know that the average temperature on Earth is going up. It is now about one degree warmer than 100 years ago. Earth is expected to get even warmer in the next century. This trend is called global warming.

Causes

Scientists think an increase in greenhouse gases is a cause for the warming trend. Gases such as carbon dioxide, methane, and nitrous oxide collect in the air. They work like the glass roof of a greenhouse. They trap heat near Earth's surface. That is why they are called greenhouse gases. Without greenhouse gases, Earth would be too cold. With too much of them, Earth would be too hot.

People burn many fossil fuels (coal, oil, and natural gas) for energy. Cars, trucks, and buses use fossil fuels. Factories and farms do, too. These fossil fuels are released into the air. This makes too much carbon dioxide and other gases. The increase in greenhouse gases makes the surface of Earth warm much faster than it would naturally.

Results

The rise in temperature on Earth is causing changes. The warmer Earth is causing ocean levels to rise. Droughts, fire, and floods are happening more often because of the warmer weather. Polar ice caps are melting.

Since 1997, leaders from many countries have been meeting in Japan to talk about global warming. The countries have worked on a plan. The goal is to reduce the use of fossil fuels that cause global warming. This way, Earth won't be so much warmer in 50 years!

Nonfiction Reading Practice, Grade 5 • EMC 3316 • ©2003 by Evan-Moor Corp.

Name _____

A Warmer Earth

Fill in the bubble to answer each question or complete each sentence.

1. Which of the following is true about Earth's temperature?
   - Ⓐ It is getting warmer.
   - Ⓑ It is getting cooler.
   - Ⓒ The temperature is staying the same.
   - Ⓓ No one knows for sure.

2. About how much warmer is it now compared with 100 years ago?
   - Ⓐ 5 degrees
   - Ⓑ 10 degrees
   - Ⓒ 1 degree
   - Ⓓ It is the same.

3. What have humans done to make Earth warmer?
   - Ⓐ They have changed the amount of sunlight.
   - Ⓑ They have burned too many fossil fuels.
   - Ⓒ They have invented a new greenhouse gas.
   - Ⓓ They have recycled products.

4. Greenhouse gases trap _____ in Earth's atmosphere.
   - Ⓐ heat
   - Ⓑ cold air
   - Ⓒ carbon dioxide
   - Ⓓ fossil fuels

5. What term is used to describe how the temperature is rising on Earth?
   - Ⓐ atmosphere
   - Ⓑ pollution
   - Ⓒ greenhouse gases
   - Ⓓ global warming

Bonus: One way to help stop global warming is to reduce the need for fossil fuels and to start using more solar energy. On the back of this page, write three other things you could do to help save energy.

Global Warming—Global Problem

The Problem

People have been saying that Earth is getting warmer. Are they right? Scientists think so, but not everyone agrees.

Studies show that the average temperature on Earth is going up. It is about one degree warmer now than 100 years ago. Earth is expected to warm several more degrees in the next 100 years. Most of this warming has happened in the last 30 years. And, 10 out of the last 15 years were the warmest years of the century. This trend is called global warming, and it is causing worldwide problems.

The Causes

Greenhouse gases that are normally in our atmosphere absorb heat. This heats up Earth's surface. Without these greenhouse gases, Earth would be too cold. But with too much of them, Earth would be too hot.

Human pollution adds higher amounts of greenhouse gases into the atmosphere. Here's what humans do:

- Carbon dioxide is released when fuels, oils, and wood are burned.
- Coal, gas, and oil emit the gas methane.
- Farms and factories emit the gas nitrous oxide.
- Ozone gases are released by manufacturing.

Pollution adds greenhouse gases to Earth's atmosphere.

The Results

Snow and ice at the poles are melting due to the warmer earth. This is causing sea levels to rise. This might lead to coastal towns being flooded.

Polar bears depend on ice fields for their food supply. They hunt seals on the ice in winter. When the ice melts, polar bears live all summer on land without food. Due to global warming, the polar bear's ice is melting too early. By 2050, up to 60 percent of the polar bears' ice may be lost.

One Solution

Since 1997, many countries have been gathering in Kyoto, Japan, to discuss global warming. The countries have worked on a plan called the Kyoto Treaty. The goal is to reduce the use of products that cause global warming.

But some countries, like the United States, are still debating whether Earth really is getting warmer. It is hard to make changes if not everyone agrees on the problem.

Nonfiction Reading Practice, Grade 5 • EMC 3316 • ©2003 by Evan-Moor Corp.

Name _____

Global Warming—Global Problem

Fill in the bubble to answer each question or complete each sentence.

1. About how much warmer is Earth now compared with 100 years ago?
   - Ⓐ It is the same.
   - Ⓑ It is 1 degree warmer.
   - Ⓒ It is 5 degrees warmer.
   - Ⓓ It is 10 degrees warmer.

2. If global warming doesn't stop, how much warmer is Earth supposed to be 100 years from now?
   - Ⓐ 10 degrees
   - Ⓑ 20 degrees
   - Ⓒ 30 degrees
   - Ⓓ several degrees

3. How have people made Earth warmer?
   - Ⓐ They have adjusted the amount of sunlight.
   - Ⓑ They have planted more trees.
   - Ⓒ They have released pollution into the air.
   - Ⓓ They have melted the ice at the poles.

4. Which group of words best describes some of the different kinds of greenhouse gases?
   - Ⓐ temperature, degrees, warming, and average
   - Ⓑ carbon dioxide, methane, nitrous oxide, and ozone
   - Ⓒ oxygen, carbon dioxide, methane, and ozone
   - Ⓓ coal, gas, oil, and fossil fuels

5. The goal of the Kyoto Treaty is to _____.
   - Ⓐ reduce the warming trend throughout the world
   - Ⓑ trap greenhouse gases
   - Ⓒ feed the polar bears
   - Ⓓ use coal, gas, and oil

Bonus: On the back of this page, explain in your own words what global warming is and possible causes for it.

Global Warming Trend

A Warmer Earth

The average temperature on Earth has increased between 0.9° and 1.6°F (0.5 and 0.9°C) in the last 100 years. Earth is expected to warm an additional 3° to 8°F (1.5 to 4.5°C) by 2100.

Most scientists think human activity has caused this warming trend. People have released pollution into the atmosphere. This pollution traps gases, and this has warmed Earth. Also, people have cut down forests worldwide. Trees remove carbon dioxide from the atmosphere. Where there are fewer trees to remove carbon dioxide, the temperature of Earth's surface goes up.

What Causes It?

Natural greenhouse gases collect in the atmosphere. They work like the glass roof of a greenhouse, trapping heat near Earth's surface. Without them, Earth would be too cold. With too much of them, Earth would be too hot. Greenhouse gases are carbon dioxide, methane, nitrous oxide, and ozone. But here's what humans do to increase these gases:

- More carbon dioxide is released when fossil fuels are burned.
- Burning fossil fuels (coal, oil, and natural gas) emits more methane gas.
- Farms and factories emit more nitrous oxide gas.
- More ozone gases are released by manufacturing.

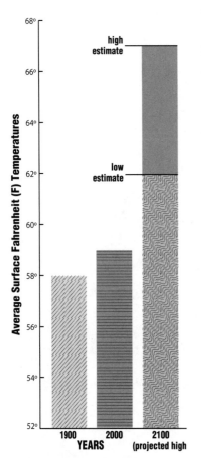

A Few Degrees—So What?

A few degrees might not seem like much. But snow and ice at the poles are melting due to warmer temperatures. Sea levels have risen. If sea levels continue to rise, coastal towns could flood.

Warmer temperatures also might allow disease-spreading insects such as mosquitoes to live farther away from the equator. Earlier springs might happen. This could change animal reproduction and migration.

Solar Energy

Greenhouse gases stay in the atmosphere for a long time. Scientists want people to make changes now. Solar energy is one solution. Burning fossil fuels gives off a lot of gases. Energy from the sun gives off no gases. Solar energy is not mined from Earth like fossil fuels. It does not pollute the air, ground, or water supply. Right now, solar energy is expensive, but scientists are finding cheaper ways to use it.

Of course, the best solution to the global warming trend is for more people to commit to using less energy in the first place.

Nonfiction Reading Practice, Grade 5 • EMC 3316 • ©2003 by Evan-Moor Corp.

Name _____

Global Warming Trend

Fill in the bubble to answer each question or complete each sentence.

1. In 100 years, the Earth's average surface temperature is expected to _____.
   - Ⓐ increase by only one degree
   - Ⓑ increase a few degrees
   - Ⓒ decrease one degree
   - Ⓓ stay the same

2. Which of the following statements is <u>not</u> true about greenhouse gases?
   - Ⓐ Greenhouse gases stay in the atmosphere for a long time.
   - Ⓑ Greenhouse gases trap heat near Earth's surface.
   - Ⓒ Without greenhouse gases, Earth would be too hot.
   - Ⓓ Carbon dioxide and methane are two greenhouse gases.

3. People burn too many fossil fuels. What are *fossil fuels*?
   - Ⓐ another name for the ozone layer
   - Ⓑ another name for greenhouse gases
   - Ⓒ oxygen and carbon dioxide
   - Ⓓ coal, oil, and natural gas

4. Why are forests needed to help reduce global warming?
   - Ⓐ Trees naturally remove carbon dioxide from the atmosphere.
   - Ⓑ Trees give people and animals shade.
   - Ⓒ Trees provide shelter for many kinds of animals.
   - Ⓓ Trees provide wood to heat people's homes.

5. Global warming has caused _____.
   - Ⓐ the sun to provide more energy for Earth
   - Ⓑ people to burn more fossil fuels
   - Ⓒ the polar ice caps to melt and sea levels to rise
   - Ⓓ the temperature of Earth's surface to fall

Bonus: Some scientists say that changes in Earth's temperature are part of a natural cycle of warming and cooling that has been going on for much of Earth's history. They don't think that human activity has caused global warming. On the back of this page, give three reasons why you think human activity has or has not caused global warming.

Measuring Length

Introducing the Topic

1. Reproduce page 127 for individual students, or make a transparency to use with a group or the whole class.

2. Tell students that the rest of the world has adopted the metric system for measurement. The United States is one of a very few countries that still uses the customary system. Show students the two systems of measuring length and discuss which one is easier to remember. Have students spend time reading and remembering the measurements. You may choose to extend the lesson by teaching students how to change the units, using the two rules at the bottom of the page.

Reading the Selections

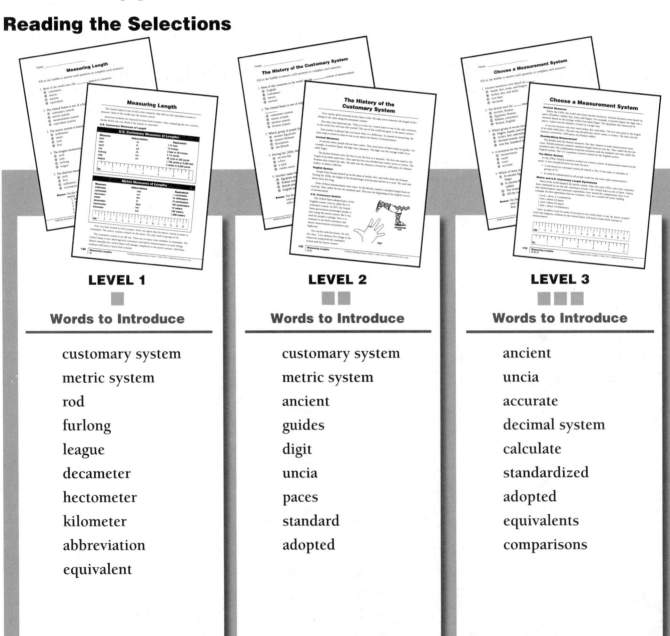

LEVEL 1	LEVEL 2	LEVEL 3
■	■ ■	■ ■ ■
Words to Introduce	**Words to Introduce**	**Words to Introduce**
customary system	customary system	ancient
metric system	metric system	uncia
rod	ancient	accurate
furlong	guides	decimal system
league	digit	calculate
decameter	uncia	standardized
hectometer	paces	adopted
kilometer	standard	equivalents
abbreviation	adopted	comparisons
equivalent		

U.S. Customary Measures of Lengths

Measure	Abbreviation	Equivalent
inch	in.	1/12 foot
foot	ft.	12 inches
yard	yd.	3 feet or 36 inches
rod	rd.	5 1/2 yards
furlong	fur.	40 rods or 220 yards
mile	mi.	1,760 yards or 5,280 feet

in. 1 2 3 4 5 6

Metric Measures of Lengths

Measure	Abbreviation	Equivalent
millimeter	mm	.1 centimeter
centimeter	cm	10 millimeters
decimeter	dm	10 centimeters
meter	m	100 centimeters
decameter	dam	10 meters
hectometer	hm	100 meters
kilometer	km	1,000 meters

cm 1 2 3 4 5 6 7 8 9 10 11 12 13 14 15

Remember these two rules:

1. To change larger units to smaller units, you multiply.

For example: 6 feet = ___ inches

3 feet × 12 (12 inches in 1 foot) = 36 inches

3 meters = ___ centimeters

3 meters × 100 (100 centimeters in 1 meter) = 300 centimeters

2. To change smaller units to larger units, you divide.

For example: 6 feet = ___ yards

6 ÷ 3 (3 feet in 1 yard) = 2 yards

3,000 meters = ___ kilometers

3,000 ÷ 1,000 (1,000 meters in 1 kilometer) = 3 kilometers

Measuring Length

The United States is one of only a few countries that still use the customary system to measure. Most of the world uses the metric system.

American students are expected to learn both systems. After comparing the two systems, decide which one you think is the easiest to remember.

U.S. Customary Measures of Length

U.S. Customary Measures of Lengths

Measure	Abbreviation	Equivalent
inch	in.	1/12 foot
foot	ft.	12 inches
yard	yd.	3 feet or 36 inches
rod	rd.	5 1/2 yards
furlong	fur.	40 rods or 220 yards
mile	mi.	1,760 yards or 5,280 feet

Metric Measures of Lengths

Measure	Abbreviation	Equivalent
millimeter	mm	.1 centimeter
centimeter	cm	10 millimeters
decimeter	dm	10 centimeters
meter	m	100 centimeters
decameter	dam	10 meters
hectometer	hm	100 meters
kilometer	km	1,000 meters

Now you have looked at both systems. Don't you agree that the metric system is easier to remember? The metric system is based on the meter. You only work in groups of 10.

The customary system is an old one. There are so many more numbers to remember. The United States is now showing both customary and metric measurements on most things. Maybe someday the United States will change completely to the metric system. Until then, students will need to learn both systems.

Nonfiction Reading Practice, Grade 5 • EMC 3316 • ©2003 by Evan-Moor Corp.

Name _____

Measuring Length

Fill in the bubble to answer each question or complete each sentence.

1. Most of the world uses the _____ system to measure.
   - Ⓐ customary
   - Ⓑ metric
   - Ⓒ ancient
   - Ⓓ equivalent

2. The United States is one of a few countries that uses the _____.
   - Ⓐ customary system
   - Ⓑ metric system
   - Ⓒ measurement system
   - Ⓓ equivalent system

3. The metric system is based on the _____.
   - Ⓐ millimeter
   - Ⓑ meter
   - Ⓒ inch
   - Ⓓ foot

4. The longest measurement of length in the customary system is the _____.
   - Ⓐ yard
   - Ⓑ mile
   - Ⓒ league
   - Ⓓ furlong

5. The shortest measurement of length in the metric system is the _____.
   - Ⓐ inch
   - Ⓑ foot
   - Ⓒ centimeter
   - Ⓓ millimeter

Bonus: On the back of this page, answer the following questions about the metric system:
   1. Would you measure your pencil using centimeters or meters?
   2. How many centimeters are in two meters?
   3. Which is longer, five meters or one kilometer?
   4. How many centimeters are in one decimeter?
   5. Which is shorter, a decameter or a hectometer?

The History of the Customary System

Your teacher gives everyone in the class a ruler. He asks you to measure the length of five things in the class using the customary system.

You raise your hand and ask, "Why is it that the United States is one of the only countries in the world that still uses this system? The rest of the world has gone to the metric system."

Your teacher is pleased that you know there is a difference. So instead of measuring, the class stops to listen to what he has to say about the history of measurement.

Ancient Measures

In ancient times, people did not have rulers. They used parts of their bodies as guides. For example, in ancient Egypt, the digit was a measure. The digit was the average width of an adult finger.

The ancient Romans were the first to use the foot as a measure. The foot was equal to the length of an adult male's foot. They said the foot was divided into twelve uncia, or inches. The Romans also created the mile. The mile was the distance covered by 1,000 paces of a Roman soldier, or about 5,280 feet.

English System

People from Europe picked up on the idea of inches, feet, and miles from the Romans. During the 1100s, the length of the British king's arm became known as a yard. The yard was about three feet long.

None of these measurements were exact. So the British created a standard length from an iron bar. They called the bar the standard yard. This was the beginning of the English system of measurement.

U.S. Customary System

The United States adopted parts of the English system. Ours is called the U.S. customary system. In 1975, the United States government encouraged people to start using the metric system. But it was hard for people to change. Now, it is common to see both customary and metric measurements on products and highway signs.

The teacher ends his lesson. He tells the class, "Let's measure five things in the classroom using both the customary system and the metric system."

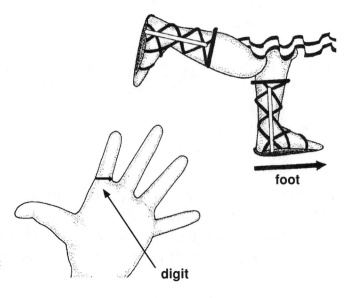

foot

digit

Name _____

The History of the Customary System

Fill in the bubble to answer each question or complete each sentence.

1. Most of the countries in the world use the _____ system of measurement.
   Ⓐ English
   Ⓑ customary
   Ⓒ metric
   Ⓓ ancient

2. The United States is one of only a few countries in the world to use
   the _____.
   Ⓐ customary system
   Ⓑ metric system
   Ⓒ ancient system
   Ⓓ Roman system

3. Which group of people first used the foot as a measure?
   Ⓐ ancient Egyptians
   Ⓑ ancient Romans
   Ⓒ Europeans
   Ⓓ the British

4. During the 1100s, the British created a new standard length using _____.
   Ⓐ an iron bar
   Ⓑ a foot
   Ⓒ a yard
   Ⓓ twelve uncia

5. Another name for the customary system of measurement is the _____.
   Ⓐ Egyptian system
   Ⓑ Roman system
   Ⓒ British system
   Ⓓ English system

Bonus: The Romans created the idea of a mile. The mile was the distance covered by 1,000 paces of a Roman soldier. On the back of this page, solve this math problem: How many feet are covered in 3,000 paces?

Choose a Measurement System

Ancient Measures

Before the 1100s, the world only knew ancient measures. Ancient measures were based on parts of bodies—hands, feet, arms, and fingers. For example, in ancient Egypt the digit was a measure based on the average width of an adult finger.

It was the Romans who first used inches, feet, and miles. The foot was equal to the length of an adult male's foot. The foot was divided into twelve uncia, or inches. The mile was the distance covered by 1,000 paces of a Roman soldier.

Standardizing Measurement

The British used the Roman measures. But they wanted to make measurement more exact. British scientists created a standard length from an iron bar. They called the bar the standard yard. The combination of ancient measures and the standard yard was called the English system. The U.S. customary system is based on the English system.

The Metric System

In the 1790s, French scientists worked out a better system of measurement based on the meter. It was considered more accurate because:

- it was based on a decimal system all related to 10s. It was easier to calculate in groups of 10.

- it could be standardized so all people could use the exact same measurements.

Metric and U.S. Customary Length Equivalents

Most of the world adopted the metric system. Since the early 1970s, only a few countries have continued to use the old, customary system—the United States is one of them. Charts that showed metric and customary equivalents were needed for comparisons. Here is an example of a few equivalents that are common. They are rounded for easier reading.

1 inch = about 2.5 centimeters
1 foot = about 0.3 meter
1 yard = about 0.9 meter
1 mile = about 1.6 kilometers

Now, wouldn't it just be easier if everyone in the world chose to use the metric system? Until that happens, students in the United States will need to learn both systems of measurement.

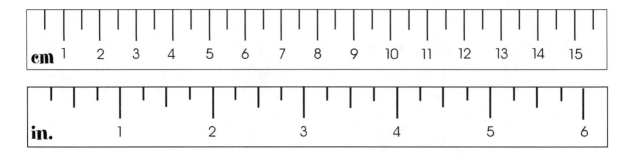

Name _____

Choose a Measurement System

Fill in the bubble to answer each question or complete each sentence.

1. Ancient measures were based on _____.
   - Ⓐ hands, feet, arms, and fingers
   - Ⓑ inches, feet, and miles
   - Ⓒ iron bars
   - Ⓓ decimals

2. The British used the _____ measures and then created their own _____ system.
   - Ⓐ ancient, Roman
   - Ⓑ Egyptian, Roman
   - Ⓒ Roman, customary
   - Ⓓ Roman, English

3. Which group of words describes the metric system of measurement?
   - Ⓐ fingers, hands, and arms
   - Ⓑ inches, feet, and miles
   - Ⓒ decimal system, meter, groups of 10
   - Ⓓ iron bar, standard length, and standard yard

4. A synonym for the word *equivalent* is _____.
   - Ⓐ measurement
   - Ⓑ equal
   - Ⓒ exact
   - Ⓓ accurate

5. Which of these statements is true?
   - Ⓐ In ancient Egypt, the digit was a measure based on the width of a child's finger.
   - Ⓑ In ancient Rome, the mile was the distance covered by 100 paces of a soldier.
   - Ⓒ The United States uses the customary system of measurement.
   - Ⓓ All the countries in the world use only the metric system of measurement.

Bonus: On the back of this page, solve the following measurement problem. Be sure to show your work. Convert how many centimeters would equal one foot. Use the comparison chart on page 132 to help you.

West African Dance

Introducing the Topic

1. Reproduce page 135 for individual students, or make a transparency to use with a group or the whole class.

2. Share with students that every culture in the world performs dances. In Africa, traditions and stories are kept in the form of music and dance. They are passed down from generation to generation. Share with students that many dance troupes travel around the country sharing the traditional West African dances. Show students the pictures of traditional West African instruments and discuss how these are both similar and different from the ones they see today.

Reading the Selections

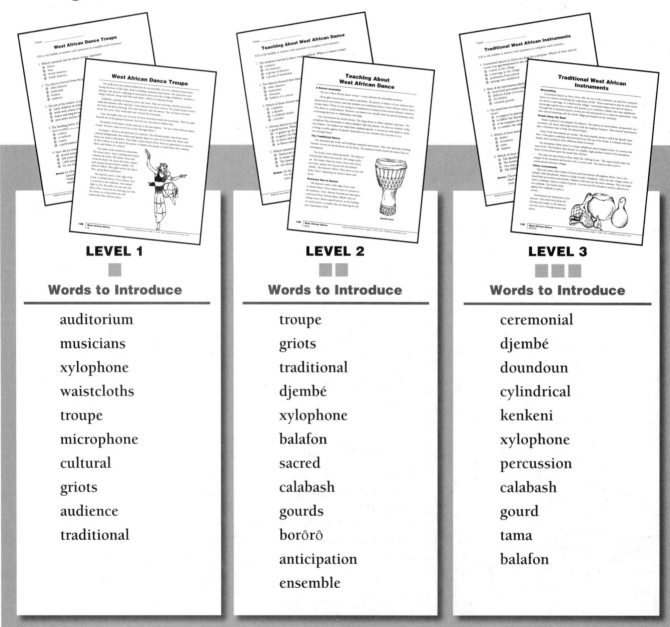

LEVEL 1 ■

Words to Introduce

auditorium

musicians

xylophone

waistcloths

troupe

microphone

cultural

griots

audience

traditional

LEVEL 2 ■ ■

Words to Introduce

troupe

griots

traditional

djembé

xylophone

balafon

sacred

calabash

gourds

borôrô

anticipation

ensemble

LEVEL 3 ■ ■ ■

Words to Introduce

ceremonial

djembé

doundoun

cylindrical

kenkeni

xylophone

percussion

calabash

gourd

tama

balafon

West African Instruments

Here are four types of traditional instruments that are used to accompany West African dance:

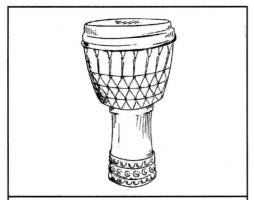

1. djembé (jem-bay)

This drum is open at both ends and has a goat or antelope skin stretched over it. It is beaten with bare hands. It is able to make three different sounds.

2. balafon (bah-lah-phone)

This is a large wooden xylophone. It is made of wooden keys attached to different sizes of calabash gourds. The gourds have tiny holes drilled into them over which special dried spider egg sacs are stretched.

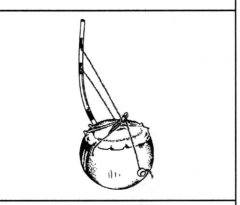

3. borôrô (boe-roe-roe)

This is a two-stringed harp. It is made from a large calabash gourd over which an antelope or goat skin is stretched. A long, curved stick is placed through the calabash. It is tightened with two strings. The strings are plucked with the fingers or with a wooden pick.

4. shaker

There is a large variety of shakers used in African music. A popular one is made from a calabash gourd. A woven net covered with beads or seeds is placed over the gourd.

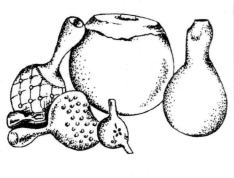

West African Dance Troupe

You walk into your school auditorium for an assembly. You see a lineup of musicians facing the front of the room. Each is holding a separate instrument. The musicians start playing. One person is playing an instrument that looks like a large xylophone. Another is using a whistle, along with bells and rattles. Others are playing drums.

Suddenly, a parade of dancers enters the room. They are wearing colorful waistcloths, ankle decorations, bells, and hats. Some dancers also have scarves. The leader heads toward the front and starts dancing. The other dancers copy his moves. They all dance forward across the room. They work their way toward the musicians.

Soon, the leader runs out of room. He bows forward toward the musicians. Then he pulls himself out of the group of dancers. Row by row, the dancers follow him.

The leader of the dance troupe steps up to the microphone. "We are a West African dance troupe. We have come to tell you a story through dance."

He begins. "Africa is divided into 53 countries. The African people come from many cultural backgrounds. But within each group, dance is a part of everyday life. Music and dance are used to tell stories. They help to pass history down from one generation to another. In West Africa, it is the job of the griots, or leaders of a group, to hand down the customs and traditions of a culture."

The leader nods toward the musicians. The music starts. Soon a pulsing movement vibrates the room. The leader turns and twists his body. He waves his arms, squats, and repeats his movements rapidly. The dancers follow. They glide across the dance floor, moving faster and faster.

The dancers come to the edge of the room. A whistle blows. Every dancer runs to a person in the audience. One dashes right to you. She pulls you out onto the dance floor. Soon you are dancing, just like the others, in a thousand-year-old traditional West African dance.

Nonfiction Reading Practice, Grade 5 • EMC 3316 • ©2003 by Evan-Moor Corp.

Name _____

West African Dance Troupe

Fill in the bubble to answer each question or complete each sentence.

1. Which continent did the dance troupe represent?
   - (A) Africa
   - (B) Asia
   - (C) North America
   - (D) South America

2. The dancers learned from the griots. What are *griots*?
   - (A) other dancers
   - (B) musicians
   - (C) leaders
   - (D) audience

3. The job of the griots is to _____.
   - (A) teach children in schools
   - (B) work with others to keep the country safe
   - (C) dance and sing for audiences
   - (D) pass down stories of African history through music and dance

4. Customs and _____ are handed down from one generation to the next.
   - (A) dancers
   - (B) traditions
   - (C) countries
   - (D) performances

5. How old are some of the traditional African dances?
   - (A) several years old
   - (B) 100 years old
   - (C) 1,000 years old
   - (D) No one knows for sure.

Bonus: In African cultures, music and dance are used to tell stories. The dancers may tell about a good harvest or a special marriage ceremony. Name three other things or events the dancers could tell about through music and dance.

Teaching About West African Dance

A School Assembly

"We are a West African dance troupe," a man informs the assembled students.

"We're glad you are here to watch us perform. The griots, or leaders, of our cultures have passed down our history, and that includes our traditional dances. Each African culture has a unique dance. What you are seeing is a combination of dances from several African countries. This dance is a performance. However, our dances are usually done for special meaning, such as blessing harvests or celebrating a marriage.

"Our instruments are mostly drums. The large drum is called a djembé (jem-bay). The xylophone-like instrument is called a balafon (bah-lah-phone). We also use whistles, bells, and shakers. The shakers are made from calabash gourds. A woven net with beads or seeds is hung to strike against the gourd. Sometimes we use a borôrô (boe-roe-roe). It is a two-stringed harp."

The Traditional Dance

The musicians get ready, each holding a separate instrument. They start playing a pulsing rhythm: rit–rit–rit–da-da-boom, da-da-boom. The audience looks toward the dance floor in anticipation.

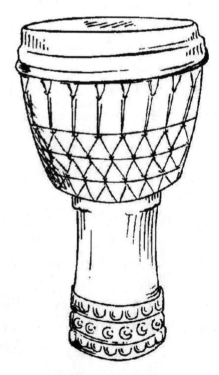

The leader starts dancing slowly. The dancers behind him follow his moves. The tempo picks up. The leader flaps his arms, turns and twists his body, squats, and repeats his movements rapidly. The dancers follow. They move across the dance floor, repeating the dances faster and faster.

Everyone Has to Dance!

The dancers come to the edge of the room. A whistle blows. Every dancer runs to a person in the audience. Soon, dozens of people are dancing a traditional West African dance. Maybe they are telling a story about a good harvest, or the healing of a sick person, or maybe they are dancing for the pure enjoyment of life.

Djembé drum

Name _____

Teaching About West African Dance

Fill in the bubble to answer each question or complete each sentence.

1. The students watched a dance troupe perform. What is a *dance troupe*?
   - Ⓐ a dancer
   - Ⓑ two dancers
   - Ⓒ a group of dancers
   - Ⓓ a group of musicians

2. The dancers learned their dances from griots. What are *griots*?
   - Ⓐ other dancers
   - Ⓑ musicians
   - Ⓒ Africans
   - Ⓓ leaders of a culture

3. Which of these African musical instruments is a drum?
   - Ⓐ a balafon
   - Ⓑ a djembé
   - Ⓒ a calabash shaker
   - Ⓓ a borôrô

4. African dances are usually done for special meaning. One celebration is for a good harvest. What does the word *harvest* mean?
   - Ⓐ to gather up the crops
   - Ⓑ to gather the family together
   - Ⓒ to heal a sick person
   - Ⓓ to bless a marriage

5. Which statement is <u>not</u> true about African dance?
   - Ⓐ Dances are usually done for special meaning.
   - Ⓑ A variety of musical instruments are used.
   - Ⓒ The dancers follow whatever the leader does in the dance.
   - Ⓓ All African cultures have the same kind of dances.

Bonus: On the back of this page, describe what an African shaker looks like. Try drawing what you think it may look like and add a caption to your picture.

Traditional West African Instruments

Storytelling

Ceremonial dances in West Africa, like the rest of the continent, are done for a purpose. Dance is a means of marking the experiences of life. Those experiences may be such events as a birth, a marriage, or a death in the village. Ceremonial dances may also be done to encourage a good crop, to heal a sick person, or to celebrate a child's entry into adulthood. Through the ceremonial dances, stories are told and passed on to each new generation. They have special meaning, and the whole village participates in the ceremony.

Drums Keep the Beat

Music is played to accompany the dancers. The dances are both athletic and graceful. In a ceremony, the music may begin slowly with the singing of praises. Then musical instruments play a rhythmic beat to help the dancers begin.

Most of the instruments are drums. The most popular drum is called the djembé (jem-bay). It has goat or antelope skin stretched over the top of the drum. It is beaten with bare hands, and it produces three different kinds of sounds.

The doundoun (dune-dune) is a large cylindrical, barrel-shaped drum. It is used as the base drum. The kenkeni (ken-kenee) is a smaller, high-pitched version of the doundoun. Both of these drums give the steady base rhythm.

The tama (ta-ma) drum is often called the "talking drum." The tama is held under the armpit of the drummer and struck with a curved stick. The tama is often used to communicate between villages.

Other Instruments

There are many other kinds of drums and instruments throughout Africa. One is the balafon (bah-lah-phone), which is a large wooden xylophone. There are also a large variety of hand-held percussion instruments. Shakers of all sizes are the most common. They are made from a calabash, which is a kind of gourd. A woven net full of beads or seeds is placed over the calabash. The beads strike against the calabash to make a sound.

Instruments are important to the dancers. They help them keep the rhythm and tempo so the dancers can tell a story through music and dance.

Name _____

Traditional West African Instruments

Fill in the bubble to answer each question or complete each sentence.

1. Ceremonial dances in Africa are done for a purpose. Which of these special events was <u>not</u> mentioned in the article?
   - Ⓐ a birth in the village
   - Ⓑ a marriage in the village
   - Ⓒ graduation from school
   - Ⓓ passage into adulthood

2. Most of the instruments played are _____.
   - Ⓐ hand-held percussion instruments
   - Ⓑ different kinds of drums
   - Ⓒ the balafon
   - Ⓓ calabash gourds

3. The musicians accompany the dancers. What does the word *accompany* mean?
   - Ⓐ to support by playing along on instruments
   - Ⓑ to follow the dancers around
   - Ⓒ to be company for the dancers
   - Ⓓ to conduct the music

4. Which of these instruments is made from a calabash gourd?
   - Ⓐ balafon
   - Ⓑ doundoun
   - Ⓒ tama
   - Ⓓ shaker

5. Which of these statements is true about West African instruments?
   - Ⓐ The djembé is the most popular drum.
   - Ⓑ The kenkeni is a larger, high-pitched version of the doundoun drum.
   - Ⓒ The tama drum is often called the "talking drum."
   - Ⓓ The balafon is a large wooden xylophone.

Bonus: Choose your favorite West African instrument from the article. On the back of this page, write three facts about it, and also explain why it is your favorite. Include a picture of the instrument.

How to Do Plays

Introducing the Topic

1. Reproduce page 143 for individual students, or make a transparency to use with a group or the whole class.

2. Point out the different pictures related to a play—the makeup, expressions, set, and costume. Tell students they are going to read about what it takes to put on a good performance for a play.

Reading the Selections

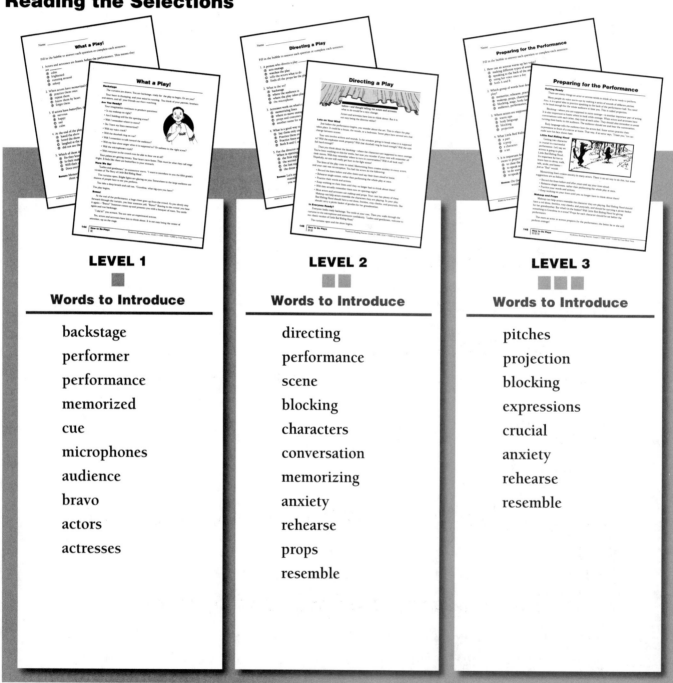

LEVEL 1

Words to Introduce

backstage

performer

performance

memorized

cue

microphones

audience

bravo

actors

actresses

LEVEL 2

Words to Introduce

directing

performance

scene

blocking

characters

conversation

memorizing

anxiety

rehearse

props

resemble

LEVEL 3

Words to Introduce

pitches

projection

blocking

expressions

crucial

anxiety

rehearse

resemble

What Makes a Play Successful!

Here are six things you need to know in order to put on a successful play. This is an example of things a group of fifth-graders needed to remember to put on the play *Little Red Riding Hood* for the kindergartners and parents.

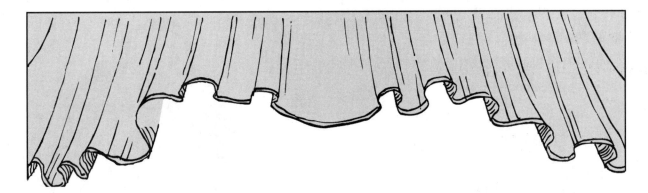

1. Get the set ready.

2. Gather up all the props.

3. Wear a costume.

4. Put on makeup.

5. Memorize, or learn the lines of the play.

6. Use expression and body language.

What a Play!

Backstage

The curtains are drawn. You are backstage, ready for the play to begin. Or are you?

Your heart is thumping, and your mind is running. You think of your parents, brothers and sisters, and all your friends out there watching.

Are You Ready?

Your imagination continues to produce questions:

- Is my makeup on right?

- Am I holding still for the opening scene?

- Will I remember where to move?

- Do I have my lines memorized?

- Will my voice crack?

- Will the doorbell ring on cue?

- Will I remember to talk toward the audience?

- Will my face show anger when it is supposed to? Or sadness in the right scene?

- Will the microphones work?

- Will everyone in the crowd even be able to hear me at all?

Your palms are getting sweaty. Your heart races faster. This must be what they call stage fright. It feels like there are butterflies in your stomach.

Here We Go!

"Ladies and gentlemen," an announcer starts. "I want to introduce to you the fifth grade's version of *The Story of Little Red Riding Hood*."

The curtains open. Bright lights are glaring on you. Somewhere in the large audience are dozens of people here to see you perform.

You take a deep breath and call out, "Grandma, what big eyes you have!"

The play begins.

Bravo!

At the end of the performance, a huge cheer goes up from the crowd. As you slowly step forward through the curtain, you hear someone yell, "Bravo!" Bowing to the crowd, you hear it again—"Bravo!" Someone comes up and presents you with a bouquet of roses. You smile again and run backstage.

"I did it!" you scream. You are now an experienced actress.

Yes, actors and actresses have lots to think about. It is not easy being the center of attention, up on the stage.

Name _____

What a Play!

Fill in the bubble to answer each question or complete each sentence.

1. Actors and actresses are *backstage* before the performance. This means they are _____.
   Ⓐ in the opening scene
   Ⓑ on center stage
   Ⓒ behind the curtain
   Ⓓ in the audience

2. When actors have *memorized* their lines, they _____.
   Ⓐ have practiced them once
   Ⓑ have repeated them
   Ⓒ know them by heart
   Ⓓ have forgotten them

3. If actors have *butterflies*, they probably are _____.
   Ⓐ nervous
   Ⓑ happy
   Ⓒ sad
   Ⓓ calm

4. At the end of the play, the crowd cheers, "Bravo!" That means they _____.
   Ⓐ hated the show
   Ⓑ loved the show
   Ⓒ laughed at the show
   Ⓓ did not see the whole show

5. Which of these do actors or actresses <u>not</u> have to think about to perform?
   Ⓐ Do they know their lines?
   Ⓑ Is their makeup on right?
   Ⓒ Will their voices be loud enough?
   Ⓓ Does everyone in the audience have a program to read?

Bonus: Memorizing lines for a play is difficult. On the back of this page, write three ways to help you remember your lines.

Directing a Play

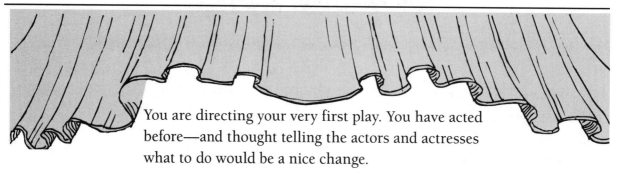

You are directing your very first play. You have acted before—and thought telling the actors and actresses what to do would be a nice change.

Actors and actresses have lots to think about. But it is not easy being the director either!

Lots on Your Mind

Just before the performance begins, you wonder about the set. This is where the play takes place. It could be a house, the woods, or a bedroom. Some plays have several sets that change between scenes.

Your sets involve actions and sounds. Is the window going to break when it is supposed to? Will the explosion work properly? Will that doorbell ring be loud enough? Will the rain fall hard enough?

Then you think about the blocking—where the characters are supposed to move onstage. You've been working on this for weeks, but now you wonder if your cast will remember all their moves. Will they remember where to turn in conversation? Will it all look real? Hopefully, no one will really get hurt in the fight scene!

The lines of the play come to mind. Memorizing lines creates anxiety in many actors, and your cast was no exception. You had the actors do the following:

- Record the lines before and after theirs and say their lines aloud at home.
- Rehearse single scenes, rather than performing the whole play at once.
- Practice their words and actions.
- Keep working on their lines until they no longer had to think about them!
- Will they actually remember them now on opening night?
- Most actors and actresses use makeup and props. Your cast has plenty of these. Makeup can help actors resemble the characters they are playing. In your play, Red Riding Hood should have a red dress, freckles, rosy cheeks, and ponytails. She should carry a picnic basket of goodies for her grandmother.

Is Everyone Ready?

Everyone looks ready backstage. You smile at your cast. Then you walk through the curtains to the microphone and announce confidently, "Ladies and gentlemen, welcome to our class's version of *Little Red Riding Hood*."

The curtains open and the show begins.

Name _____

Directing a Play

Fill in the bubble to answer each question or complete each sentence.

1. A person who directs a play _____.
   - Ⓐ acts onstage
   - Ⓑ watches the play
   - Ⓒ tells the actors what to do
   - Ⓓ finds all the props for the play

2. What is the *set*?
   - Ⓐ backstage
   - Ⓑ where the audience is
   - Ⓒ where the play takes place
   - Ⓓ the microphone

3. Actresses work on what's called blocking. *Blocking* is _____.
   - Ⓐ memorizing lines
   - Ⓑ where to move onstage
   - Ⓒ props and costumes
   - Ⓓ another name for *set*

4. What is a good way to memorize lines?
   - Ⓐ Say them only once.
   - Ⓑ Practice them over and over.
   - Ⓒ Practice lines and actions.
   - Ⓓ Both B and C are good.

5. For the director and actors, opening night is both exciting and nerve-racking.
   When is *opening night*?
   - Ⓐ the first night of the performance
   - Ⓑ the second night of the performance
   - Ⓒ the last night of the performance
   - Ⓓ the dress rehearsal

Bonus: Let's say you are going to play the Big Bad Wolf. How could you
resemble the wolf? On the back of this page, write all the things that
you would do to prepare for this part.

Preparing for the Performance

Getting Ready

There are many things an actor or actress needs to think of to be ready to perform.

Many people do voice warm-ups by making a series of sounds of different pitches. Also, it is a good idea to practice speaking to the back of the performance hall. You need to be loud enough for the whole audience to hear you. This is called projection.

Blocking—where you are supposed to move onstage—is another important part of acting. It is also important to know where to look while onstage. When actors and actresses have conversations with each other, they look at each other. They should also remember to avoid turning their backs to the audience. The audience should see and hear the conversation.

Body language tells the audience how the actors feel. Some actors practice their expressions in front of a mirror at home. That way, if an actor says, "I hate you," he can make sure his face shows hate.

Little Red Riding Hood

Getting into character is crucial to a successful performance. Let's say an actress is going to play Little Red Riding Hood. It's important for her to know how to dress, walk, talk, smile, and listen— just as "Red" would.

Memorizing lines creates anxiety in many actors. There is no set way to do this, but some suggestions are as follows:

- Record the lines before and after yours and say your lines aloud.
- Rehearse single scenes, rather than performing the whole play at once.
- Practice your words and actions.
- Keep working on your lines until you no longer have to think about them!

Makeup and Props

Makeup can help actors resemble the character they are playing. Red Riding Hood should have a red dress, freckles, rosy cheeks, and ponytails, and should be carrying a picnic basket for her grandmother. But what's in the basket? Will Little Red Riding Hood be giving something to Grandma in a scene? Props for each character should be set before the performance.

The more an actor or actress prepares for the performance, the better he or she will perform onstage!

Name _____

Preparing for the Performance

Fill in the bubble to answer each question or complete each sentence.

1. How can an actress warm up her voice?
   - Ⓐ making different types of sounds
   - Ⓑ speaking to the back of the audience
   - Ⓒ using her voice once a day
   - Ⓓ both A and B

2. Which group of words best describes what it takes to remember lines in a play?
   - Ⓐ memorize, rehearse, practice
   - Ⓑ makeup, props, character
   - Ⓒ blocking, stage, body language
   - Ⓓ audience, performance, scenes

3. Where actors are supposed to move onstage is called _____.
   - Ⓐ warm-ups
   - Ⓑ body language
   - Ⓒ blocking
   - Ⓓ projection

4. What Little Red Riding Hood carries in her basket is called _____.
   - Ⓐ a part
   - Ⓑ a prop
   - Ⓒ a character
   - Ⓓ a set

5. It is important for actors and actresses to project their voices. What does it mean to *project*?
   - Ⓐ to clear the throat
   - Ⓑ to speak softly
   - Ⓒ to do warm-ups
   - Ⓓ to speak loud enough for the whole audience to hear

Bonus: On the back of this page, write a paragraph about why you would or would not like to be a professional actor or actress.

Charles Schulz

Introducing the Topic

1. Reproduce page 151 for individual students, or make a transparency to use with a group or the whole class.

2. Ask students what they think is the most famous comic strip. Then share with them that the answer is *Peanuts*. Ask them if they know the name of the creator of *Peanuts*. Share with them that it is Charles Schulz. Show students the time line of Charles Schulz.

Reading the Selections

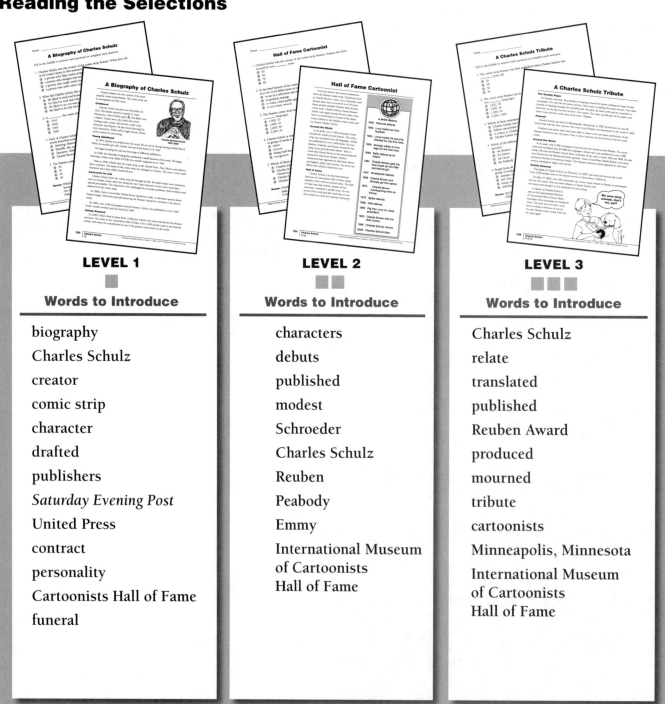

LEVEL 1	LEVEL 2	LEVEL 3
Words to Introduce	**Words to Introduce**	**Words to Introduce**
biography	characters	Charles Schulz
Charles Schulz	debuts	relate
creator	published	translated
comic strip	modest	published
character	Schroeder	Reuben Award
drafted	Charles Schulz	produced
publishers	Reuben	mourned
Saturday Evening Post	Peabody	tribute
United Press	Emmy	cartoonists
contract	International Museum of Cartoonists Hall of Fame	Minneapolis, Minnesota
personality		International Museum of Cartoonists Hall of Fame
Cartoonists Hall of Fame		
funeral		

Time Line of Charles Schulz

1922 — Schulz was born on November 22 in Minneapolis, Minnesota.

1940 — Schulz graduated from high school in St. Paul, Minnesota.

1943 — Schulz was drafted into the army and served in armored infantry in Europe during World War II.

1948 — Sold his first cartoon to *Saturday Evening Post*.

1950 — United Press Syndicate bought his originally named comic strip *Lil Folks*. Renamed it *Peanuts*.

1955 — Awarded the National Cartoonists Society's Reuben Award.

1957 — Rhinehart Company began releasing *Peanuts* comic strips in books. Schulz's comics eventually sold in over 1,400 different books.

1965 — *Peanuts* made its television debut as a cartoon special.

1967 — Broadway play *You're a Good Man Charlie Brown* opened.

1984 — *Peanuts* appeared in over 2,300 newspapers and in 40 languages.

1999 — Retired from drawing. By this time, Schulz had won another Reuben award, a Peabody award, and Emmys.

2000 — Died February 13 in Santa Rosa, California. Later, over 100 cartoonists ran comic strips related to *Peanuts*. This was a tribute to Schulz and 50 years of *Peanuts*.

A Biography of Charles Schulz

Charles Schulz was the creator of the popular comic strip *Peanuts*. The comic strip ran in newspapers for fifty years.

Charles Monroe Schulz
1922–2000

Childhood

Charles Schulz was born on November 22, 1922. His family moved to nearby St. Paul, Minnesota, where Schulz grew up. His father was a barber. Schulz was a shy child who loved reading comic strips. His favorite comic strip character was Popeye. He also loved drawing his own characters. While still in high school, Schulz took a course in cartooning.

Young Adulthood

In 1943, Schulz was drafted into the army. He served in Europe during World War II. When his mother got sick, Schulz was sent back home to St. Paul.

He began sending his cartoon drawings to different publishers. In 1948, the *Saturday Evening Post* published a small amount of his work. He began drawing a comic strip called *Lil Folks* in a weekly magazine in St. Paul.

Then in 1950, Schulz sent the comic strip to the United Press. They liked it and offered him a contract. The name of the comic strip was changed to *Peanuts*. The comic strip's main character was a boy called Charlie Brown.

Cartoonist for Life

Charles Schulz drew the comic strip all through his life. He added many new characters such as Snoopy, Linus, and Lucy along the way. Each character in his comic strip had a special personality. The characters were challenged by everyday problems. Both children and adults loved the comic strip.

In the 1960s, *You're a Good Man Charlie Brown* opened as a play. A television special about *Peanuts* began. Television specials featuring the *Peanuts'* characters continue to be shown today.

By 1984, over 2,300 newspapers carried *Peanuts*. Schulz was published in over 1,400 books. Schulz worked until he retired in 1999.

Schulz Honored

In 2,000, Schulz died in Santa Rosa, California. Schulz won many awards for his *Peanuts* cartoons. He is also in the Cartoonists Hall of Fame. Over 2,500 people came to his funeral. Schulz will always be remembered as one of the greatest cartoonists in the world.

Nonfiction Reading Practice, Grade 5 • EMC 3316 • ©2003 by Evan-Moor Corp.

Name _____

A Biography of Charles Schulz

Fill in the bubble to answer each question or complete each sentence.

1. Charles Schulz was the creator of the comic strip *Peanuts*. What does the word *creator* mean in this sentence?
   Ⓐ a person who likes comic strips
   Ⓑ a person who designs and makes a comic strip
   Ⓒ a person who reads comic strips
   Ⓓ a person who sells comic strips to newspapers

2. What did Charles Schulz like to do as a child?
   Ⓐ He liked to read and draw cartoon characters.
   Ⓑ He liked to read and ride his bike.
   Ⓒ He liked to act out war games.
   Ⓓ He liked to be like his father.

3. In _____, the comic strip *Peanuts* was first published.
   Ⓐ 1943
   Ⓑ 1948
   Ⓒ 1950
   Ⓓ 1960

4. Each of Charles Schulz's characters had a unique personality. Which group of words describes someone's personality?
   Ⓐ drawing, illustrating, and publishing
   Ⓑ likeable, shy, and talented
   Ⓒ character, child, and adult
   Ⓓ Charlie Brown, Linus, and Snoopy

5. The *Peanuts* comic strip ran in over 2,300 newspapers for _____ years.
   Ⓐ 20
   Ⓑ 30
   Ⓒ 40
   Ⓓ 50

Bonus: Which *Peanuts* character is your favorite—Charlie Brown, Linus, Lucy, Snoopy, or Woodstock? Maybe you like another one that is not mentioned. On the back of this page, write about your favorite character from the *Peanuts* comic. Be sure to give three reasons why you like that character.

Hall of Fame Cartoonist

Everyone knows the cartoon characters from the *Peanuts* comic strip. Characters such as Charlie Brown, Linus, Lucy, Schroeder, and Snoopy have been around for over 50 years. Many people consider *Peanuts* their favorite comic strip. Charles Schulz created *Peanuts*. Schulz won many awards for his comic strip. To the right is a brief history of some of the major events related to the *Peanuts* comic strips and its creator Charles Schulz.

Around the World

At its peak, over 2,300 newspapers from around the world carried *Peanuts*. The comic strip was translated into 40 languages. Schulz was published in over 1,400 books. He won Reuben, Peabody, and Emmy awards for his comic strip and television shows. *You're a Good Man Charlie Brown* is the most-produced musical in American theater. Schulz's characters have appeared in television shows, newspapers, plays, and movies. Toy stores are filled with Schulz's characters, too.

Hall of Fame

Charles Schulz is in the International Museum of Cartoonists Hall of Fame. Many samples of his work are posted there. The Hall of Fame says that Schulz, despite all his successes, remained a modest man. He was proud of his work and left word that no one else would ever draw his beloved characters.

A Brief History

1950 *Peanuts* debuts.

1952 Lucy holds her first football.

1954 Linus holds his security blanket for the first time.

1956 Snoopy walks on two legs for the first time.

1959 Sally debuts as an infant.

1961 Charlie Brown gets his first crush on the little red-haired girl.

1967 Woodstock debuts.

1969 Charlie Brown and Snoopy go into space.

1973 *A Charlie Brown Thanksgiving* wins an Emmy.

1975 Spike debuts.

1989 Olaf debuts.

1990 Pig Pen runs for class president.

1993 Charlie Brown hits his first homer.

1999 Charles Schulz retires.

2000 Charles Schulz dies.

Nonfiction Reading Practice, Grade 5 • EMC 3316 • ©2003 by Evan-Moor Corp.

Name _____

Hall of Fame Cartoonist

1. Charles Schulz was the creator of the comic strip *Peanuts. Peanuts* has been around for over _____ years.
   Ⓐ 50
   Ⓑ 60
   Ⓒ 70
   Ⓓ 80

2. In the Brief History of the comic strip, each cartoon character debuts. What does the word *debut* mean as used in this article?
   Ⓐ to act in a television special
   Ⓑ to perform onstage
   Ⓒ to make a first public appearance
   Ⓓ to win many awards

3. The *Peanuts* comic strip has appeared in over _____ newspapers and in _____ languages.
   Ⓐ 1,400; 10
   Ⓑ 1,600; 10
   Ⓒ 2,000; 40
   Ⓓ 2,300; 40

4. Charles Schulz is remembered in the Cartoonists Hall of Fame. Which word or group of words is a synonym for the word *fame*?
   Ⓐ talent
   Ⓑ success
   Ⓒ being well known
   Ⓓ recognition

5. Which of these statements is <u>not</u> true about Charles Schulz?
   Ⓐ Charles Schulz created the comic strip *Peanuts*.
   Ⓑ Charles Schulz wanted other people to continue to draw his famous characters.
   Ⓒ Charles Schulz won numerous awards.
   Ⓓ Charles Schulz is honored in the Cartoonists Hall of Fame museum.

Bonus: Charles Schulz was honored many times over his lifetime. On the back of this page, write what honor you think Schulz would have been most proud of and why.

A Charles Schulz Tribute

The Sunday Paper

It's Sunday morning. Your family is hanging around the house reading the huge Sunday newspaper. You dad has the sports section. Your mom is reading the travel section. Your older brother is flipping through the classified ads. You pick up what is left and are surprised to find that no one has the best section—the comics. You open up this part of the paper, and there's your favorite comic strip of all time—*Peanuts*.

Peanuts

Charles Schulz was born in Minneapolis, Minnesota, in 1922. By the time he was 26, Schulz had sold his first cartoon. His comic strip *Peanuts* was introduced to the world in 1950.

Children and adults alike have been able to relate to the successes and failures of the *Peanuts* characters over the years. That is why it became the best known of all the comic strips.

Around the World

At its peak, over 2,300 newspapers from all over the world carried *Peanuts*. The comic strip was translated into 40 different languages. Schulz also was published in over 1,400 books. He won the Reuben Award (best cartoonist of the year) in both 1955 and 1964. He also won Emmys for his *Peanuts* television specials. *You're a Good Man Charlie Brown* is the most-produced musical in American theater. The *Peanuts* characters have appeared in television shows, newspapers, plays, and movies.

Schulz Honored

The death of Charles Schulz on February 13, 2000, was mourned around the world. Over 2,500 people came to the funeral service in Santa Rosa, California.

On May 27, 2000, over 100 cartoonists ran comic strips related to *Peanuts* in newspapers all over the world. This was their tribute to Charles Schulz and the many years he gave to the profession of cartooning.

A tribute to Charles Schulz is also in the International Museum of Cartoonists Hall of Fame. Many examples of his drawings are displayed there. The only way the comic strip lives on today is because of reruns. No new *Peanuts* comic strips will ever be made again.

We sure miss Snoopy, don't we, pal?

Nonfiction Reading Practice, Grade 5 • EMC 3316 • ©2003 by Evan-Moor Corp.

Name _____

A Charles Schulz Tribute

Fill in the bubble to answer each question or complete each sentence.

1. The comic strip *Peanuts* was introduced to the world when Charles Schulz was _____ years old.
   Ⓐ 26
   Ⓑ 28
   Ⓒ 33
   Ⓓ 42

2. The comic strip *Peanuts* ran in over _____ newspapers and was translated into _____ languages.
   Ⓐ 1,922; 26
   Ⓑ 1,950; 26
   Ⓒ 2,300; 40
   Ⓓ 2,300; 1,400

3. Which of these statements is <u>not</u> true about Charles Schulz?
   Ⓐ Charles Schulz was born in Santa Rosa, California.
   Ⓑ Fellow cartoonists honored Charles Schulz.
   Ⓒ A tribute to Charles Schulz is in the Cartoonists Hall of Fame.
   Ⓓ Charles Schulz was published in over 1,400 books.

4. Which of the following awards was given to Charles Schulz for his television specials?
   Ⓐ the Reuben
   Ⓑ the Emmy
   Ⓒ the Oscar
   Ⓓ the Peabody

5. People from all over the world have shown tribute to Charles Schulz. Which group of words relates to the word *tribute*?
   Ⓐ attempt, success, and failure
   Ⓑ sell, buy, and publish
   Ⓒ honor, respect, and thanks
   Ⓓ well known, famous, and celebrity

Bonus: On the back of this page, create your own comic strip to pay tribute to Charles Schulz and the *Peanuts* comic strip.

Seattle's Space Needle

Introducing the Topic

1. Reproduce page 159 for individual students, or make a transparency to use with a group or the whole class.

2. Show students the diagram of Seattle's Space Needle. Notice the height and levels to the Needle. Ask them if they have ever been to Seattle, Washington, to see the Needle. Ask students if they have any ideas about how it was built and why it was built the way it is.

Reading the Selections

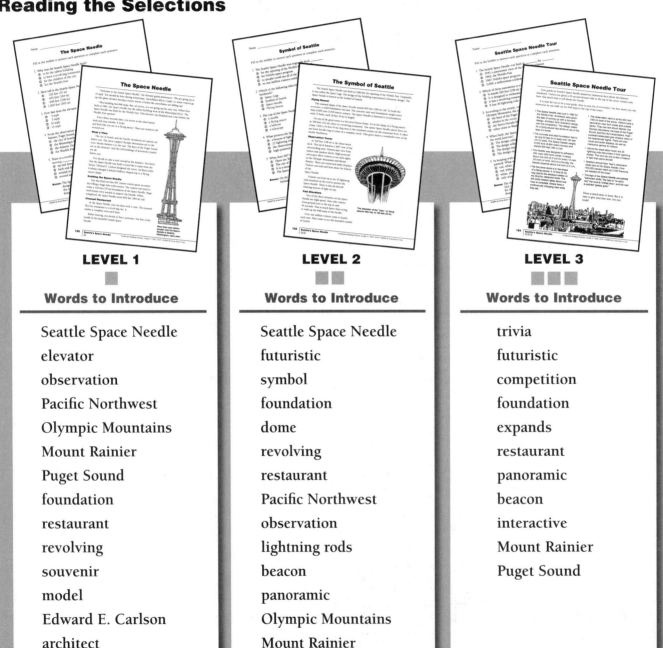

LEVEL 1

Words to Introduce

Seattle Space Needle

elevator

observation

Pacific Northwest

Olympic Mountains

Mount Rainier

Puget Sound

foundation

restaurant

revolving

souvenir

model

Edward E. Carlson

architect

LEVEL 2

Words to Introduce

Seattle Space Needle

futuristic

symbol

foundation

dome

revolving

restaurant

Pacific Northwest

observation

lightning rods

beacon

panoramic

Olympic Mountains

Mount Rainier

LEVEL 3

Words to Introduce

trivia

futuristic

competition

foundation

expands

restaurant

panoramic

beacon

interactive

Mount Rainier

Puget Sound

Seattle's Space Needle

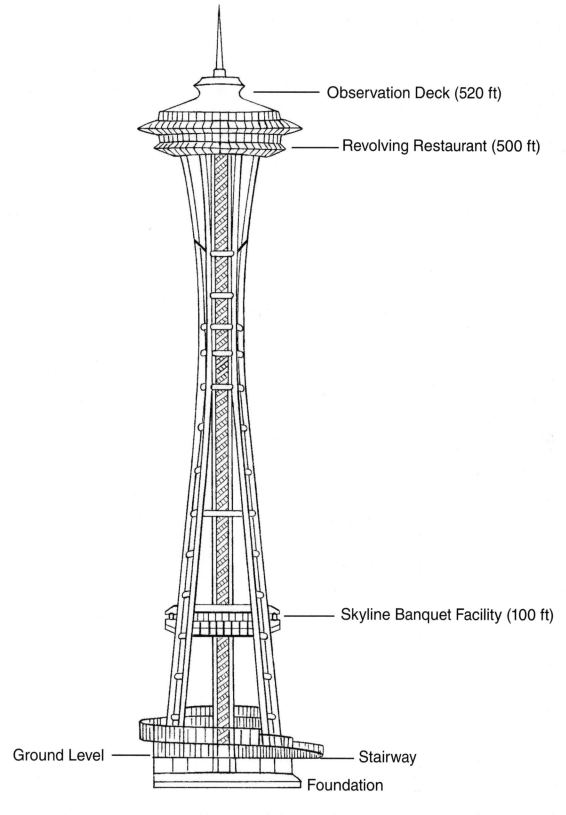

Observation Deck (520 ft)

Revolving Restaurant (500 ft)

Skyline Banquet Facility (100 ft)

Ground Level

Stairway

Foundation

The Seattle Space Needle is 605 feet (184 m) tall. It is called the Symbol of Seattle.

The Space Needle

"Welcome to the Seattle Space Needle," the elevator guide announces. "We are going up at 10 mph. You should be here during wintertime. Snowflakes fall at 3 mph. So when visitors go up this glass elevator during a winter storm, it looks like snowflakes are falling up!

"This building has 848 steps. But, of course, you are going up the easy way. When first built in 1962, the Space Needle was the tallest building west of the Mississippi River. The Space Needle was built for the World's Fair. This elevator was finished just a day before the World's Fair opened."

Forty-three seconds later, you arrive at the observation deck and step outside. It looks and feels like you are in a flying saucer. There are windows all around you.

What a View

The city of Seattle and the Pacific Northwest are spread out before you. The snow-capped Olympic Mountains are to the west. Mount Rainier is to the east. The bays of the Puget Sound are in the distance. And the tall buildings of downtown Seattle are all below you.

You decide to take a look around at the displays. You learn that the Space Needle was built to look like it came from the future. Edward E. Carlson designed the tower. Architect John Graham changed Carlson's balloon-shaped top to a flying saucer shape.

Building the Space Needle

You also find out that 467 cement trucks spent an entire day filling a huge hole with cement. The cement was used to make a 120-foot (37-m) foundation for the Space Needle. Huge steel beams were needed to support the Needle. When completed, the Space Needle stood 605 feet (184 m) tall.

Unusual Restaurant

At the Space Needle, you can dine with a view. The unusual SkyCity restaurant is a revolving one. It makes a complete turn each hour.

Before leaving, you decide to buy a souvenir. You buy a tiny model of the beautiful Seattle Space Needle.

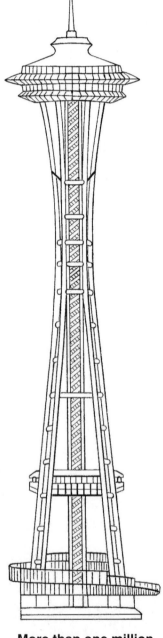

More than one million people visit the Space Needle in Seattle, Washington, each year.

Nonfiction Reading Practice, Grade 5 • EMC 3316 • ©2003 by Evan-Moor Corp.

Name _____

The Space Needle

Fill in the bubble to answer each question or complete each sentence.

1. Why was the Seattle Space Needle built?
   - Ⓐ to be the tallest building
   - Ⓑ to have a revolving restaurant
   - Ⓒ for the children of the city
   - Ⓓ for the World's Fair

2. How tall is the Seattle Space Needle?
   - Ⓐ   120 feet (37 m)
   - Ⓑ   605 feet (184 m)
   - Ⓒ   848 feet (258 m)
   - Ⓓ 1,000 feet (305 m)

3. How fast does the elevator move as it takes people to the observation deck?
   - Ⓐ   3 mph
   - Ⓑ   5 mph
   - Ⓒ 10 mph
   - Ⓓ 15 mph

4. From the observation deck, visitors can see the Olympic Mountains, Mount Rainier, Puget Sound, and _____.
   - Ⓐ the city of Seattle
   - Ⓑ the Mississippi River
   - Ⓒ the Atlantic Ocean
   - Ⓓ the World's Fair

5. There is a revolving restaurant at the Space Needle. The word *revolving* means moving _____.
   - Ⓐ up and down
   - Ⓑ back and forth
   - Ⓒ around in a circle
   - Ⓓ around in a half circle

Bonus: The Space Needle was built with a flying saucer-like top. What other design might have worked? On the back of this page, write about what the top of your design would look like. Include a drawing of your new design.

The Symbol of Seattle

The Seattle Space Needle was built in 1962 for the opening of the World's Fair. Originally, it was called the Space Cage. The design of the building represented a futuristic design. The Space Needle is known as the Symbol of Seattle.

Flying Saucer

The unusual shape of the Space Needle stands 605 feet (184 m) tall. To build the structure, a solid foundation was laid. The concrete and steel foundation weighs more than 6,000 tons (5,443 metric tonnes). The Space Needle is fastened to its foundation with 72 bolts, each 30 feet (9 m) in length.

On top of the great tower is a five-level house dome. It's in the shape of a flying saucer. At 500 feet (152 m), there is a revolving restaurant. The entire Space Needle saucer does not rotate. Only a 14-foot (4-m) ring next to the windows rotates on the restaurant level. It takes one hour for the ring to rotate in a complete circle. This gives diners a wonderful view of the Pacific Northwest.

Observation Tower

At 520 feet (158 m) is the observation deck. This deck features a 360° view of the surrounding area. Visitors may view from indoor and outdoor decks. High-powered telescopes allow visitors to see such sights as the Olympic Mountains and Mount Rainier. There are visual and audio displays. Visitors can read and hear about the history of the Space Needle.

Visitors can look up to see 25 lightning rods attached on the roof to protect the Space Needle. There is also an aircraft warning beacon of light on top.

Fast Elevators

Two of the three elevators on the Space Needle are high speed. They take visitors from ground zero to the top in only 43 seconds. That is much faster than trying to walk up the 848 steps of the Needle.

Over one million visitors come to Seattle each year. They come to see this beautiful symbol of Seattle.

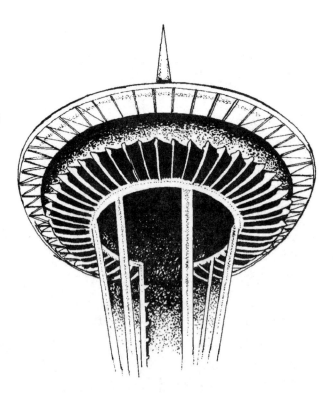

The diameter of the "halo," or flying saucer-like top, is 138 feet (42 m).

Name _____

The Symbol of Seattle

Fill in the bubble to answer each question or complete each sentence.

1. The Seattle Space Needle was originally built _____.
   - Ⓐ for the opening of the World's Fair in 1962
   - Ⓑ for NASA's space program
   - Ⓒ so people could see all of the Pacific Northwest
   - Ⓓ so one million visitors could visit the landmark

2. Which of the following titles has <u>not</u> been given to Seattle's most famous landmark?
   - Ⓐ Space Cage
   - Ⓑ Symbol of Seattle
   - Ⓒ Space Needle
   - Ⓓ Flying Saucer

3. The top of the Space Needle is shaped like _____.
   - Ⓐ a needle
   - Ⓑ a flying saucer
   - Ⓒ a balloon
   - Ⓓ a telescope

4. What protects the Space Needle from thunderstorms?
   - Ⓐ a beacon of light
   - Ⓑ 25 lightning rods
   - Ⓒ the observation deck
   - Ⓓ high-powered telescopes

5. What does 360° mean?
   - Ⓐ There are 360 steps to the top of the Space Needle.
   - Ⓑ The city of Seattle is 360 miles away.
   - Ⓒ It is a measurement of a complete circle in degrees.
   - Ⓓ The Space Needle was originally supposed to be 360 feet tall.

Bonus: On the back of this page, design a brochure for the Space Needle. Include at least five facts about the Needle and a picture.

Seattle's Space Needle Tour

Tour guides at Seattle's Space Needle memorize numerous facts about this famous landmark. Visitors are given a 43-second elevator ride to the top of the tower. Guides only have that much time to tell about the Needle.

It is time for you to be a tour guide. Here is your list of trivia facts. See how many you can memorize as you walk up the 848 steps to the top of the tower.

- The Space Needle was built in 1962 for the World's Fair. Architects were given the task of coming up with a futuristic design. Architect John Graham's design won the competition. The design called for a flying saucer-like dome on top of the legs of a tower.

- The concrete and steel foundation had to be dug 30 feet (9 m) deep and 120 feet (37 m) wide. The Space Needle weighs 9,550 tons (8,664 metric tonnes) and stands 605 feet (184 m) tall.

- The Needle was designed to withstand 200-mph (320-kmh) winds. It sways about one inch (2.5 cm) for every 10 mph (16 kmh) of wind. And on a hot day, the Needle expands about one inch (2.5 cm).

- The five-level dome is in the shape of a flying saucer. A 14-foot (4-m) ring next to the windows rotates on the SkyCity restaurant level. The full-circle rotation takes about one hour to complete. Diners have a continuously changing view while they eat.

- The observation deck is at the 520-foot (158-m) level of the dome. Visitors have a panoramic view from inside and outside decks. They can see Mount Rainier, the Olympic Mountains, the bays of the Puget Sound, and the city's skyscrapers. High-powered telescopes give closeup views of the spectacular sights.

- Above the observation tower are 25 lightning rods that protect it from lightning strikes. The very top one is also a beacon of light that warns aircraft.

- Seattle's annual New Year's celebration takes place at the Space Needle. Over 400,000 people watch as 2,000 fireworks are blasted off the tower.

- The legs of the Space Needle are painted "astronaut white," the halo is "re-entry red," the core is "orbital olive," and the roof is painted "galaxy gold."

There is much more to learn. But it is time to give your first tour. Are you ready?

Name _____

Seattle's Space Needle Tour

Fill in the bubble to answer each question or complete each sentence.

1. The Seattle Space Needle was built in _____ for _____.
   Ⓐ 1943; a panoramic view of the Pacific Northwest
   Ⓑ 1962; the World's Fair
   Ⓒ 1967; NASA's space program
   Ⓓ 2,000; a millennium celebration

2. Which of these statements is true about the Space Needle?
   Ⓐ It stands 520 feet (158 m) tall.
   Ⓑ It is designed to withstand up to 100-mph winds.
   Ⓒ It has a revolving restaurant that rotates a full circle every hour.
   Ⓓ It has 30 lightning rods on top of the tower.

3. According to the article, visitors can see such sights as Mount Rainier, the Olympic Mountains, the city of Seattle, and _____.
   Ⓐ the bays of the Puget Sound
   Ⓑ whales in the ocean
   Ⓒ the Sierra Nevada Mountains
   Ⓓ other cities in Washington

4. When built, the Space Needle had a futuristic design. Which sentence describes the word *futuristic*?
   Ⓐ The design called for a dome on top of steel legs.
   Ⓑ The design called for the modern-day materials of steel and concrete to be used.
   Ⓒ The design represented the history of Seattle.
   Ⓓ The design represented looking ahead to the next century of progress.

5. In keeping with the futuristic theme of the World's Fair, the Space Needle was painted. What were the colors used on the Space Needle?
   Ⓐ red, white, and blue
   Ⓑ red, white, yellow, and green
   Ⓒ white, olive, red, and gold
   Ⓓ only white

Bonus: The theme of the 1962 World's Fair was the future and looking ahead to the 21st century. You have been asked to design a building for the World's Fair for the next century. On the back of this page, plan and draw your new design. Be sure to give it a name and write three interesting facts about it.

Name _____

Write the important details of the famous person's life.

Who [ ]

Where [ ]

Sketch

Where (he/she lives or lived)

_____

_____

_____

_____

_____

_____

What (he/she does or did)

_____

_____

_____

_____

_____

_____

Why (it is important to know about him/her)

_____

_____

_____

_____

_____

_____

166

Name _____

KWL Chart

Before reading the article, write what you already know about the topic. Write what you want to know about the topic. After you finish reading the article, write what you learned about the topic.

Topic:		
K	**W**	**L**
What I **K**now	What I **W**ant to Know	What I **L**earned

Name _____

Making an Outline

As you read the article, take notes on three important main ideas or subtopics. After you have read the article, write the title of the article. Write three subtopics as main headings (I–III) in the outline. Write each subtopic's details (A–C) in the outline.

_____
Title of article

I. _____

   A. _____

   B. _____

   C. _____

II. _____

   A. _____

   B. _____

   C. _____

III. _____

   A. _____

   B. _____

   C. _____

Name _____

Multisection Web

Use this web to write the main idea and supporting details for three important paragraphs in the article.

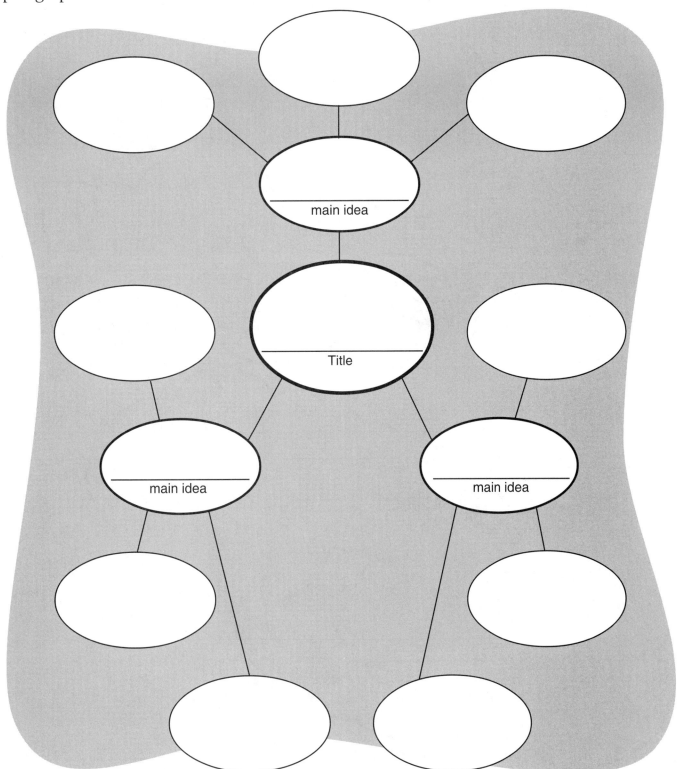

Name _____

Sequence Chart

Use this chart to sequence the events in the article.

Name _____

Vocabulary Quilt

As you read the article, write new words and their meanings in the quilt squares.

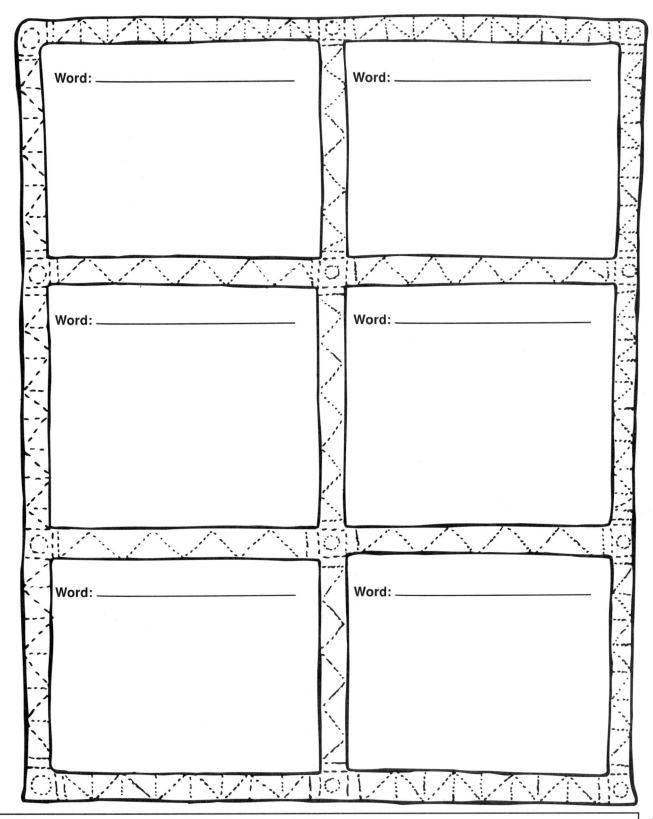

Answer Key

page 9
1. A
2. B
3. D
4. C
5. A

Bonus: Answers will vary, but the picture of Stonehenge should include a circular pattern of large stones. The caption may include such facts as: built 5,000 years ago, built in a circular pattern, stones weighed about 50 tons (45 metric tonnes), or other ideas from the article.

page 11
1. C
2. A
3. D
4. B
5. C

Bonus: Answers will vary. Students may choose one of the three reasons listed or give an original idea as long as they support their answer.

page 13
1. A
2. C
3. B
4. C
5. D

Bonus: Answers should include the following steps: Holes were dug for two stones. Teams of men used great levers and ropes to raise each stone into place. A horizontal stone lintel was laid across the pillars.

page 17
1. D
2. B
3. C
4. A
5. B

Bonus: Answers should include that Hiawatha wanted peace between all the Iroquois tribes so they could be united into one powerful nation.

page 19
1. A
2. B
3. C
4. D
5. B

Bonus: Answers should include that the Iroquois' villages were destroyed and they were forced to live on reservations in different areas.

page 21
1. B
2. D
3. B
4. A
5. C

Bonus: Answers will vary, but might include the fact that this league was the first democratic system used in the United States. The founding fathers used some of the Iroquois League's ideas in writing the Bill of Rights.

page 25
1. C
2. B
3. D
4. C
5. B

Bonus: Answers will vary, but should include the idea that Shackleton risked his own life to go get help for his men. He rescued all his men off Elephant Island.

page 27
1. B
2. D
3. C
4. A
5. D

Bonus: Answers will vary, but might include ideas such as: blizzards, freezing temperatures, windy, deserted, food ran out, and men were getting sick and suffered from frostbite.

page 29
1. C
2. D
3. C
4. C
5. B

Bonus: Answers will vary, but might include such things as: abandoning the ship, using lifeboats to get to Elephant Island, leaving men behind while he went for help, or waiting three months for the weather to clear up before returning to Elephant Island.

page 33
1. C
2. D
3. A
4. B
5. B

Bonus: Answers will vary, but might include the idea that the Native Americans were defending their families and way of life. Other ideas might be that the warriors outnumbered the soldiers, or that Reno and Benteen retreated rather than helping Custer.

page 35
1. B
2. A
3. C
4. D
5. C

Bonus: Answers will vary, but might include the idea that this was the last time Custer fought the Native Americans. The word *stand* refers to supporting an issue in a clear and forceful way. Custer believed it was his duty to stand up against the Native Americans and forcefully remove them so settlers could take over the lands.

page 37
1. B
2. C
3. A
4. C
5. D

Bonus: Answers will vary, but should include the idea that it was the army that led an attack on the Sioux and Cheyenne.

page 41
1. C
2. D
3. A
4. C
5. B

Bonus: Answers will vary, but should include that many volcanoes and earthquakes happen along the Ring of Fire.

page 43
1. C
2. B
3. D
4. A
5. D

Bonus: Answers will vary, but students should choose one of the three—an earthquake, a volcanic eruption, or a tsunami. Students should give reasons to support their answer. For example: Earthquakes do the most damage. More than 80,000 earthquakes shake the area each year. Earthquakes can cause tsunamis to happen.

page 45
1. D
2. B
3. A
4. D
5. C

Bonus: Answers will vary, but should include that the earth is divided into tectonic plates. The plates bump into each other. One plate sinks beneath the other plate. The grinding movements cause earthquakes and volcanoes. Many tectonic plates surround the Ring of Fire area, so this is why there is so much earthquake and volcanic activity.

page 49
1. D
2. C
3. A
4. B
5. C

Bonus: Answers should include the two rules stated in the question. Number 1 rule should show N and S pulling toward each other. Number 2 rule should show two like poles (N and N, or S and S) pushing away from each other.

page 51
1. C
2. C
3. D
4. A
5. B

Bonus: Answers will vary, but should include some of the following facts: They are temporary magnets. To make an electromagnet, electricity goes through a coil of wire that has been wrapped around an iron or steel core. It only attracts metal objects while an electric current is on. Electromagnets are in such things as doorbells, refrigerators, washing machines, CD players, and many other appliances.

page 53
1. C
2. A
3. D
4. B
5. C

Bonus: Answers will vary, but students should include either a permanent (bar, horseshoe, round, or cylinder) or a temporary magnet (electromagnet) in their design.

page 57
1. D
2. A
3. B
4. C
5. A

Bonus: Answers should include the following steps: 1. Buy brine shrimp eggs. 2. Add eggs to salty warm water. 3. When eggs hatch, give shrimp yeast as food.

page 59
1. C
2. B
3. C
4. A
5. B

Bonus: Answers will vary, but possible facts might include: They are crustaceans. They have an exoskeleton. They live in salty lakes and ponds. They eat algae and bacteria. Brine shrimp eggs can live for years without hatching. Brine shrimp can be bought and raised at home. Sea Monkeys are a kind of brine shrimp. Mono Lake is home to trillions of brine shrimp.

page 61
1. C
2. D
3. C
4. A
5. D

Bonus: This is a two-step problem. First, students divide 90 days by 4 days, which equals 22.5 days. Then students must multiply 22.5 x 100, which equals a total of 2,250 cysts.

page 65
1. B
2. A
3. C
4. D
5. D

Bonus: The picture and captions should include the sun shining on Earth, a water source such as the ocean, water vapor rising, tiny water droplets forming in clouds, and then rain falling to Earth.

page 67
1. B
2. C
3. A
4. D
5. A

Bonus: Answers will vary, but answers might include: The good news is that there is always the same amount of water on Earth, and countries are working together to solve water problems. The bad news is that world populations are growing, and so is the need for more water. People are not conserving enough, and they are also polluting the water supplies.

page 69
1. D
2. C
3. A
4. B
5. C

Bonus: Answers will vary, but ideas might include: taking a shower instead of a bath; turning off the tap while brushing teeth, washing hands, or washing the car; putting in plants that are native and don't need as much water; and fixing leaky faucets and toilets.

page 73
1. B
2. D
3. C
4. A
5. D

Bonus: Answers will vary, but the picture should include: clouds in the sky, an airplane dropping chemicals from above the cloud. Water droplets form in the cloud and then it starts to rain on Earth. The caption might include one of the sentences from the learning visual.

page 75
1. C
2. A
3. B
4. D
5. A

Bonus: Answers will vary, but ideas might include: Too much rain may cause flooding. Too much rain might ruin crops. Putting chemicals in the clouds may make the water polluted.

page 77
1. A
2. C
3. D
4. B
5. A

Bonus: Answers will vary, but students should realize that the amount of water remains the same. The problem is that the world's population is increasing, and so is the need. Cloud seeding helps to increase the amount of water as needed.

page 81
1. B
2. C
3. D
4. A
5. B

Bonus: Answers will vary, but students should describe a natural setting such as a national park, the woods, an ocean, a river, or a prairie meadow.

page 83
1. C
2. D
3. C
4. B
5. A

Bonus: Answers will vary, but students might mention the national parks he helped—Yosemite and Grand Canyon. They may write that Muir worked with President Roosevelt and the Sierra Club to help preserve the natural areas that became national parks.

page 85
1. A
2. B
3. C
4. B
5. D

Bonus: Answers will vary, but students might include ideas such as: They practice the 3R's (reduce, reuse, and recycle). They may clean up parks, conserve water, and participate in school and community environmental projects.

page 89
1. C
2. C
3. B
4. D
5. A

Bonus: Answers will vary, but students should include ABC steps on their poster.

page 91
1. D
2. B
3. C
4. C
5. B

Bonus: Answers will vary, but students should mention four things. These may include such things as: Limit sun exposure from 10:00 a.m. to 4:00 p.m. Wear sunscreen with an SPF of 15 or higher. Wear protective clothing and sunglasses. Be careful around sand, water, or snow because they reflect the sun.

page 93
1. D
2. B
3. A
4. D
5. B

Bonus: Answers will vary, but students should mention that dangers of too much sun lead to skin problems, premature aging, and skin cancer. Protection from the sun includes such things as wearing sunscreen, light-colored clothing, hats, and sunglasses.

page 97
1. D
2. B
3. A
4. C
5. A

Bonus: Answers will vary, but students should emphasize the need to wear the most important piece of equipment—a helmet.

page 99
1. C
2. B
3. B
4. C
5. A

Bonus: Answers will vary, but students should emphasize the idea that it is cooler to wear a helmet than to be injured or killed in a biking accident. Designs on bike helmets help them to look cooler.

page 101
1. D
2. C
3. B
4. D
5. A

Bonus: Answers will vary, but students should include four statistics. Statistics may include: 28 million children ride bikes; 300,000 get medical treatment from bike accidents; 9,000 are hospitalized; and about 4,500 children have serious head injuries. Only 15% to 25% of children wear helmets. And only 19 states have bike helmet laws.

page 105
1. D
2. A
3. B
4. C
5. D

Bonus: Answers will vary, but students should include ideas such as: After the accident, Wellman worked hard to get back to climbing. He designed special tools to help him climb. He helped other disabled athletes to succeed, too.

page 107
1. A
2. C
3. B
4. A
5. D

Bonus: Students should mention such things as: Worked at Yosemite National Park, developed special equipment for disabled athletes, climbed Yosemite's Half Dome and El Capitan, did downhill skiing and white-water kayaking, sit-skied across a mountain range, wrote a book about his life, made outdoor videos, and started his own company.

page 109
1. C
2. B
3. D
4. A
5. B

Bonus: Answers will vary, but students should include three questions that were not answered in the article. Questions may include: What was it like to be in the wilderness alone, waiting to be rescued? What are some of the adaptive climbing tools you have designed? Next to rock climbing, what is your favorite sport? What was it like to be honored at the Paralympics in 1996?

page 113
1. D
2. C
3. A
4. B
5. C

Bonus: Answers will vary. A reasonable answer might include: singles = 30, doubles = 12, triples = 4, home runs = 12, for a total of 58 hits.

page 115
1. A
2. D
3. C
4. B
5. B

Bonus: Answers will vary, but should be reasonable. Batting averages should range from a low of about 0.200 to a high of about 0.400. An example of a reasonable batting average might be: AB = 72, 1B = 9, 2B = 8, 3B = 1, HR = 3, for a total of 21 hits. This batting average is 0.292.

page 117
1. D
2. B
3. C
4. C
5. A

Bonus: Answers should be accurate. Students add the hits for a total of 156. They divide 156 by 476 to get a 0.3278 average for 2001. According to the article, Bonds' average in 2002 was 0.370, so 2002 was his best season.

page 121
1. A
2. C
3. B
4. A
5. D

Bonus: Answers will vary, but students might include such things as: walk or bike instead of drive, buy natural products with less packaging, plant more trees, and set up a recycling program at home and at school.

page 123
1. B
2. D
3. C
4. B
5. A

Bonus: Answers will vary, but students should mention that global warming is an increase in Earth's surface temperature. They should mention that human activity has increased greenhouse gases in the atmosphere, which cause higher temperatures.

page 125
1. B
2. C
3. D
4. A
5. C

Bonus: Answers will vary, but most students will probably choose the fact that human activity has caused global warming. Students might include reasons such as: the burning of fossil fuels; farms, factories, and manufacturing plants emitting gases; and the cutting down of forests.

page 129
1. B
2. A
3. B
4. C
5. D

Bonus: Answers must be accurate. **1.** centimeters **2.** 200 cm **3.** 1 km **4.** 10 cm **5.** decameter

page 131
1. C
2. A
3. B
4. A
5. D

Bonus: Answers must be accurate. This is a two-step problem. **1.** 1,000 pages = 1 mile, so 3,000 paces = 3 miles. **2.** There are 5,280 feet in one mile. So, 5,280 feet x 3 miles = 15,840 feet.

page 133
1. A
2. D
3. C
4. B
5. C

Bonus: The answer must be accurate. This is a three-step problem. Remind students that the answer to the conversion will be close, but not an exact answer.

1. 1 in. = about 2.5 cm

2. 12 in. = 1 ft.

3. 2.5 cm x 12 in. = 30 cm

page 137
1. A
2. C
3. D
4. B
5. C

Bonus: Answers will vary. They may include such things as: a birth, a death, a child's entry into adulthood, a new leader is named, or the rains are coming.

page 139
1. C
2. D
3. B
4. A
5. D

Bonus: Answers should mention that shakers are made from calabash gourds. There is a beaded or seeded woven net over the gourd. The beads or seeds strike against the gourd to make a sound. Students should include a picture and a caption.

page 141
1. C
2. B
3. A
4. D
5. B

Bonus: Answers will vary. Students should choose from the djembé, doundoun, kenkeni, tama, balafon, or a shaker. Three facts and a reason why it is their favorite instrument, as well as a picture, should be included.

 Nonfiction Reading Practice, Grade 5 • EMC 3316 • ©2003 by Evan-Moor Corp.